W°

HOW TO CUT YOUR TAX BILL

HOW TO CUT YOUR TAX BILL

SAVING TAX THROUGHOUT YOUR LIFETIME

Walter Sinclair

ORION

First published in Great Britain in 1995 by
Orion
An imprint of Orion Books Ltd
Orion House, 5 Upper St Martin's Lane, London WC2H 9EA

A CIP catalogue record for this book is available
from the British Library

ISBN 1 85797 645 2

Typeset by Selwood Systems, Midsomer Norton

Printed in Great Britain by
Butler & Tanner Ltd, Frome and London

To Margaret
Support of more than 30 years

Contents

Preface

Tax Planning

Only a very few people might not mind paying more tax than they need. This book is to help the others pay less. It is about tax planning.

The taxes covered are mainly direct ones, particularly income tax, capital gains tax and inheritance tax. Corporation tax is touched on, as are social security contributions. However, indirect taxes are outside the orbit of this book, so there is little mention of value added tax.

Tax planning aims at the maximisation of your after-tax income and capital for the benefit of yourself and normally your family. You will find no descriptions of complicated artificial tax-avoidance schemes. These are for the brave, who are willing to take risks on their outcome. Naturally, tax evasion is out.

If you are an adviser, you should find the chapters useful in dealing with clients. Otherwise, the book is not intended to replace your accountant or solicitor, but rather to increase your understanding of the tax planning opportunities available. This will help you better to understand their advice.

Background Information

Full explanations are given, so that no prior knowledge is needed. I do this in the seven main planning chapters. Also, I start with three 'background' chapters. The first deals generally with aspects relating to tax planning. For example, the likelihood of tax change is looked at, illustrated by a 25-year retrospect.

The second and third chapters consider the main taxes involved. Income tax is covered in Chapter 2, with a word about corporation tax. Chapter 3 covers capital taxes and in particular capital gains tax and inheritance tax.

There are also tax tables, a glossary and an index at the end of the book. However, I must emphasise that a comprehensive picture of the UK tax system is not given; only enough to understand the various tax-saving suggestions.

Full cross-referencing is used throughout, so that you are clearly directed to the main treatment of each subject. The margins are used for this purpose, among other things.

Perhaps of more importance, you will become better able to put forward your own suggestions. In this way, your tax saving strategy will be closer to your particular needs and philosophy.

The Seven Ages

A large part of the book deals with the concept of planning your tax affairs according to the particular stage that you have reached in your life. I have considered seven ages, as did Shakespeare in *As You Like It*. These are:

Childhood
Student days
Early working life
Newly married
Parenthood
Middle age
Retirement

The book has separate chapters devoted to each of the seven 'ages'. Thus you can refer to those of particular interest to you. However, you could well find yourself turning to several chapters, where for instance you have children and are concerned that your parents' affairs are properly planned.

Budget Changes

Chapter 4 is devoted to considering the November 1994 Budget provisions and related planning opportunities. Also, various Budget changes are noted throughout the book.

Acknowledgements

Tax planning is largely a family matter, so it is fitting that I acknowledge here the help and encouragement that I have received from my own. My sincere thanks to Margaret, Julian, Debra and Emma; Robert Halle and John Sinclair.

Walter Sinclair
February 1995

PART ONE

Background and Basics

No man in this country is under the smallest obligation, moral or other, so to arrange his legal relations to his business or to his property as to enable the Inland Revenue to put the largest possible shovel into his stores.

Lord Clyde, 1929

CHAPTER ONE

Tax Planning –
The Whys and Wherefores

1.1

'Never mind the whys and wherefores', said W. S. Gilbert. However, before getting down to details, let us consider some of the background to tax planning. Is it legal? How far should you go? What about complicated arrangements and anti-avoidance rules? Is it always in your best interests and good for your family?

These are some of the matters considered in this chapter. Also illustrated is the need to be aware of the way that the taxes constantly change.

1.2   What is Tax Planning?

Professor Joad in the BBC's *Brains Trust* often used to preface his answers with, 'It all depends what you mean by ...': How true for the subject of this book.

Certainly 'It' does not mean tax evasion. That is illegal and could result in your paying interest and penalties in addition to tax. You should always observe the compliance rules and make full disclosure of your income and capital gains, as required.

However, you are entitled to plan your affairs so that your own and your family's tax is reduced. This is called tax avoidance and the matters covered by this book would broadly come within this heading.

Tax planning is perfectly legal. Various court cases have made this clear.

For example, in the 1935 case of Commissioners of Inland Revenue v. Duke of Westminster, Lord Tomlin said, 'Every man is entitled if he can so to order his affairs that the tax attaching under the appropriate Acts is less than it otherwise would be.'

That case also supported the 'form' of transactions rather than their substance. That is to say, how the documents are drafted and the effect of each individual part of a scheme, rather than the overall result. Not surprisingly, highly sophisticated arrangements were devised, whose steps satisfied the Taxes Acts but which would be caught if considered as a whole.

The Inland Revenue strongly resisted such schemes and eventually managed to obtain court decisions requiring a closer look at the 'substance'. Examples are W. T. Ramsay Ltd v. CIR (1981) and Furniss v. Dawson (1984).

Complicated artificial schemes are not dealt with in this book. If you have an exceptionally large tax liability looming up, you may be tempted to investigate such a scheme, but you should only do so after taking top level professional advice. Then, be prepared for years of controversy with the Inland Revenue and possibly litigation.

So that is what is meant by tax planning, for the purposes of this book. It must be legal and not consist of evasion. Basically, it is a matter of using the many reliefs provided by the tax rules and operating within the legislation, avoiding artificial arrangements.

1.3   Anti-Avoidance Rules

As well as tax avoidance being resisted through the courts, much complicated legislation has been brought in over the years. Examples are given at the end of the next chapter. In general, you should consult your accountants and other professional advisers about tax planning. They should certainly have regard to the anti-avoidance rules where appropriate.

See 2.23

One of the problems with anti-avoidance legislation is that it may bite in quite innocent cases. A matter of throwing away the baby with the bath water. Another drawback is that some of the rules are difficult to interpret, even in the light of relevant case decisions. This is another reason to steer clear of artificial schemes.

1.4 Your Team

Tax planning could be looked on as a team sport. But you have the most at stake and you are the captain. The purpose of this book is to equip you for that task. That is not to say that you should refuse the advice of your accountant or solicitor. Rather, you should be able to understand what might be done and initiate action if necessary.

If you have an accountant, he is the best placed to advise on your tax planning. He should have an overall picture of your business affairs and often your family. You may well wish him to co-ordinate dealing with your other advisers. If you deal with your own tax return, whilst your knowledge of tax may be better, you are likely to need extra advice on tax planning.

Your solicitor may also be involved in your general tax planning. In any event, you will be wise to involve him in matters such as your will, trust deeds and property transfers. Also, if any complex legal points arise, a barrister might be consulted.

Life assurance and pensions have a very important part to play in tax planning. So your respective advisers in those fields are members of your team.

Depending on the circumstances, stockbrokers, banks and building societies may come into play on matters such as investments and loans. Furthermore, estate agents may be needed for property valuations in some cases.

The above are some of those who may be members of your team. Some may be brought in to play only occasionally, but it is important to be properly advised.

1.5 Family Matters

A lot of the tax planning in this book concerns families and transferring income and capital from one member to another. This raises a number of vital questions.

If you are considering transfers to your spouse, is your marriage sound and likely so to remain? Otherwise, think again.

Should you wish to make an outright gift to your child, is he or she sufficiently mature to deal with it? If not, consider a trust.

The question of gifts to your adult children is a much vexed one. You may fear that they will delay pursuing their careers and waste their time. However, it may enable them to take up less remunerative but highly worthwhile careers, for which they are well suited. Thus a substantial gift could be an investment in their future happiness. Again, trusts may be preferable to outright gifts, particularly if the split between family members has not yet been decided.

Then there is the vital question of your position as the giver. First, can you afford it? You should ensure that you and your spouse will have enough money for your retirement. However, if yours is a happy and trustworthy family, should you pass down too much, no doubt the children will stand by you.

Of course, some self-made men and women pass nothing down to their children in their lifetimes. 'I had no money given to me and so I shall give nothing to my children. They must stand on their own feet.' Since you are reading this book, you are unlikely to come into that category. In such cases, only the Treasury benefit. They reap a substantial inheritance tax harvest.

In short, much depends upon your own philosophy. There are no hard and fast rules as to what you should pass down, nor what other tax planning steps you take. Once you have a tax liability, this must be paid, but there are no laws that if tax is avoidable, it must be saved. However, this book suggests many ways in which tax can be saved and it is for you to choose.

1.6   The Ever-Changing Tax Scene

One of the main spurs to tax planning is that the system constantly changes. Over the past 25 years, taxes have been introduced and withdrawn. Tax rates and reliefs have been changed time and again. Hardly a year has passed without significant alterations.

However, there is at least one piece of comfort for the tax planner: retrospective legislation is frowned upon. Thus anything done when a particular tax rule applies would not normally be taxed differently as the result of later changes in the legislation.

Tax is a political football and is liable to be changed regularly, particularly in the light of economic problems. However, our present tax system is comparatively lenient. This facilitates tax planning and now is the time to put the plans into practice.

One of the best ways of judging what tax changes we may have in the future, both under the present Government and a future one, is to examine what happened previously. The next pages cover some of the changes in the last 25 years.

1.7   Income Tax

Also see 2.1– 2.19

Before the tax year 1973–4, there was a standard income tax rate of latterly 38.75% and a graduated surtax broadly on the excess over £2,000 at extra rates of up to 50%. Then, in the cause of simplification, 1973–4 saw the start of the unified tax system. The standard rate became a 30% basic rate, followed by a string of higher rates as follows:

1.8 Income tax rates for 1973–4

Slice of income after reliefs (£)	Rate (%)	Total income (£)
5,000	30	5,000
1,000	40	6,000
1,000	45	7,000
1,000	50	8,000
2,000	55	10,000
2,000	60	12,000
3,000	65	15,000
5,000	70	20,000
The remainder	75	

These rates applied to earned income. Investment income apart from the first £2,000 carried an extra 15%, making a top rate of 90%. Even considering that a pound then was worth more like six pounds in today's money, those were really steep tax rates. But for 1974–5, the highest rate became 83%, which meant a top rate of 98% on investment income.

The 98% top rate continued through 1978–9. Whilst it lasted, you only kept two pounds out of every one hundred of your investment income, once you reached the top of the rate scale. No wonder there was a surge in tax-avoidance activity and artificial schemes became so popular.

1979–80 saw the top rate come down to 60% together with a 15% investment income surcharge. This was removed after 1983–4, so that the fiscal discrimination against investment income ended. In turn, this changed tax-planning strategy.

Even more dramatically, for 1989–90 onwards there was simply a 25% basic rate and a 40% higher rate band, with a 20% lower rate appearing for 1992–3. The scale for 1994–5 is:

1.9 Income tax rates for 1994–5

Slice of income after reliefs (£)	Rate (%)	Total income (£)
3,000	20	3,000
20,700	25	23,700
The remainder	40	

The dramatic changes are strikingly shown by considering the top income tax rates on earned and investment income over the years:

1.10 Top income tax rates

Tax year	Top rate on earned income (%)	Top rate on investment income (%)
1973–4	75	90
1974–5	83	98
1978–9	83	98
1979–80	60	75
1984–5	60	60
1988–9	40	40
1994–5	40	40

1.11   Capital Gains Tax

Also see 3.1– 3.21

The most striking change regarding capital gains tax was its introduction in the first place. Apart from a short-lived tax on short-term gains, there had been no capital gains tax prior to 7 April 1965. Thus, capital profits normally had been regarded as tax free. Hence the introduction of capital gains tax required a total change in strategy.

Capital gains tax started at a flat rate of 30%, which lasted for individuals right through until 6 April 1988. From that date, gains are charged at your income tax rates of up to 40%.

However, the impact of the tax has been reduced by various reliefs. One of the most important is indexation relief. This operated on a limited basis from 6 April 1985 and now is generally taken on the value of your asset at 31 March 1982, or its cost if later. The intention is that the element of your gain due to inflation is not taxed.

One of the most important capital gains tax areas for tax planning is the treatment of gifts. Essentially, where assets are gifted, they must be treated as if sold at market value. Capital gains tax is computed on that basis. However, relief was introduced, allowing giver and recipient to elect for the gain to be held over until the latter disposed of the asset.

Gifts elections at first only applied to business assets and shares in family trading companies. From 5 April 1980, a more general gifts relief applied. However, from 14 March 1989, the scope was narrowed to broadly business assets, family trading company shares and transactions regarding certain trusts. Clearly, these changes were vital regarding tax planning.

Also see 3.22– 3.34

1.12   Inheritance Tax and its Predecessors

Wealthy individuals often can make the most spectacular tax savings in the field of what were, at one time, called death duties. However, there have been many changes, affecting the rules, rates, reliefs and actual systems.

Prior to 27 March 1974, estates passing on death were subjected to estate duty at rates starting at 25% and reaching 75% at £1,000,000.

Then came capital transfer tax, applying not only on death, but also to the gifts made each year, subject to certain exemptions. The rates went up to 75% at first, although from 10 March 1981, the top lifetime rate went down to 50%. More strikingly, the top rates became 30% and 60% from

13 March 1984. Even so, capital transfer tax remained a formidable strait-jacket for the tax planner.

But relief was at hand in the form of inheritance tax. This came in from 18 March 1986 and most lifetime gifts are now regarded as potentially exempt transfers. These are now only taxed if death occurs within seven years.

Transactions taxable during your lifetime, such as regarding discretionary settlements, are only charged at half of the full rate. At first the full inheritance tax rate was 60%, but since 15 March 1988, it has been 40%, with currently the first £150,000 being free of charge.

Thus the tax climate for gifts and bequests has become much brighter. This is shown by the following summary of the top rates over the years.

1.13 Top Estate Duty, Capital Transfer Tax and Inheritance Tax Rates

		Lifetime gifts (%)	*On Death (%)*
Estate duty pre	27 March 1974	nil*	75
Capital transfer tax from	27 March 1974	75	75
Capital transfer tax from	10 March 1981	50	75
Capital transfer tax from	18 March 1984	30	60
Inheritance tax from	18 March 1986	30**	60
Inheritance tax from	15 March 1988	20**	40

* some 'inter vivos' gifts included with estate on death.
** only of limited application.

Some very broad examples of tax changes in the last 20 or so years have been given above. What general guidelines can be drawn? Certainly tax rates have shown a marked tendency to be higher under a Labour Government than the Conservatives. At least this applies to what are known as 'direct taxes', such as income tax, capital gains tax and inheritance tax. These are in fact the main taxes dealt with in this book.

However, the Conservatives have removed or reduced some very beneficial reliefs over the years, including:

First year allowances on plant and machinery
Initial allowances on industrial buildings
Mortgage interest relief
Deed of covenant payments to students, grandchildren, etc.
Stock relief
Life assurance premium relief on post-13 March 1984 policies
Business Expansion Scheme Investments (replaced by lower Enterprise Investment Scheme).

So the message is that no tax goodies can be expected to last for ever. You should take advantage of them whilst you have the chance, provided it is sensible to do so.

1.14   Tax-Planning Guidelines

This chapter has dealt with some general background to tax planning, its meaning, your team of advisers, family matters and the way that taxes constantly change. In conclusion, here are some common-sense guidelines, which are mainly drawn from matters already discussed.

• The tax planning tail must not be allowed to wag the financial dog. In other words, your tax planning must fit in with your business and other financial objectives.

• Your tax savings must not result from, and be wiped out by, business and other losses.

• Do not cause unhappiness to your family and yourself in order to save tax. For example, do not move overseas to a country you do not like.

• Make sure that you have regard to the future financial security of your spouse and yourself when you make gifts.

• Carefully consider whether your children and grandchildren are yet mature enough to receive larger outright gifts. It may be better to establish trusts for them.

• Do not segregate income and capital in your plans. The tax treatment has been coming closer together and both need attention.

• Have regard to the likelihood that tax rules will change in the future.

Therefore avoid if possible schemes which will take a long time to reach fruition. Critical tax rules may have changed in the meantime.

● Steps to save tax should not be delayed, since they could be blocked by rule changes. Provided you can afford the tax-planning arrangements and they make sense regardless of whether or not the law changes, do not delay.

CHAPTER TWO

Tax on Income –
Some Basic Rules

2.1 Introduction

This and the next chapter are included on the principle of 'better the devil you know'! in other words, if you are setting out to save tax, it certainly helps to know a few basic details about it.

It may be that you already possess a good all-round knowledge of the subject. In that case, go on to the later chapters. Otherwise, you are recommended to spend a little time with these.

This chapter mainly deals with income tax, with a little space devoted to tax on companies. Chapter 3 covers capital taxes; in particular capital gains tax and inheritance tax. The details given refer to tax year 1994–5 unless otherwise stated.

Indirect taxes are not covered by this book and so nothing is included about value added tax. National insurance contributions are not considered at this stage either. However, both appear in the tax rates section towards the end of the book and the same applies to stamp duty.

Remember that this chapter only deals with basics and is by its nature condensed. The rules relating to specific tax-saving situations are dealt with in more depth later.

2.2   Who Is Taxable?

Residents of the United Kingdom are taxable on their income arising here. *See*
They are also liable to tax on overseas income according to the rules. *2.21–2*
Those covered include individuals, partnerships, companies, trusts and
estates.

Non-residents may also be liable to tax on their UK income. However,
they are not normally liable to capital gains tax.

Inheritance tax is payable for individuals domiciled here and for others,
broadly only on their UK assets.

2.3   The Taxes Payable

The following is a list of the taxes covered:

Income tax at rates for individuals of 20%, 25% and 40%
*See 2.5
et seq*

Capital gains tax at 20%, 25% and 40% for individuals
*See 3.2
et seq*

Corporation tax for companies on income and capital gains at 33% (25% for
companies with smaller profits)
*See
2.24–6*

Inheritance tax on wealth passing on death and in some other cases at 40%
(first cumulative £150,000 tax free).
*See 3.22
et seq
1995–6
£154,000*

2.4   Classes of Income

Your income is taxed according to the rules relating to the various
'Schedules' and 'Cases' into which it falls. These are:

Schedule A   Income from land and buildings – rents, premiums, etc.
See 2.16

Schedule C   Income payable in the UK on Gilt-Edge securities and certain
              overseas public revenue dividends

Schedule D   Case I Trades
              Case II Professions and vocations
See 2.18

15

See
2.15.5
Case III Interest annuities, etc.

Cases IV & V Overseas income from investments, possessions and businesses, etc.

Case VI Miscellaneous profits and other income not within the other cases

See 2.17 *Schedule E* Wages and salaries from employments

Case I The employee is normally UK resident

Case II Where a non-resident does work in UK

Case III UK resident works abroad and remits money to UK, but excluding income taxed under Cases I or II

See
2.15.1 *Schedule F* Dividends and certain other company distributions.

2.5 Income Tax Assessment and Payment

You are assessed to income tax for each tax year ending 5 April on your total income less allowances. The income is of the above categories and deductions are allowed as outlined below. [Your tax returns would normally provide details.]

As is seen later in this chapter, the income is sometimes that actually arising in the tax year. Sometimes it is assessed on a preceding year basis. This normally applies for trades and professions, although the basis is changing for 1996–7 and subsequently. Also from 1996–7, a self-assessment system is being introduced, under which you will be able to calculate and submit your own tax liabilities.

Income tax is normally payable on 1 January in the tax year for which it is assessed, or if later, 30 days after your assessment is issued. However, your tax on business profits (Schedule D Cases I & II) is payable in equal instalments on 1 January and 1 July. Income tax at higher rates on taxed income is payable on 1 December following the tax year. Overdue tax attracts interest at currently 6.25% (from 6 October 1994), but so do overpayments, subject to the rules.

2.6 Income Tax Rates 1994–5

See 4.2 for 1995–6

The income tax rates payable for the tax year ended 5 April 1995 are:

Taxable income band £	Tax rate %	Total income £	Total tax £
3,000 (0–3,000)	20	3,000	600
20,700 (3,000–23,700)	25	23,700	5,775
Remainder	40		

2.7 Personal Reliefs

You can claim certain personal tax reliefs for each tax year. These are deducted from your income in arriving at the taxable amount.

Husbands and wives have their own sets of allowances, since their tax is separately computed. In addition, there is a *married couple's* allowance which goes to the husband unless his income is insufficient. However, an election can be made for it to be split equally or go entirely to the wife.

The following table gives brief details of the available personal reliefs.

<table>
<tr><td>*1995–6 where changed*</td><td colspan="3">**2.8 Personal Reliefs For 1994–5**</td></tr>
<tr><td></td><td>*Type*</td><td>*When it applies*</td><td>*Relief (£)*</td></tr>
<tr><td>*3,525*</td><td>Personal allowance</td><td>In most cases unless age allowance obtained</td><td>3,445</td></tr>
<tr><td></td><td>Additional personal allowance for children</td><td>For single parents etc. not entitled to married couple's allowance</td><td>1,720*</td></tr>
<tr><td></td><td>Blind person's allowance</td><td>Registered blind person</td><td>1,200</td></tr>
<tr><td>*4,630*
4,800</td><td>Age allowance</td><td>Age 65–74</td><td>4,200</td></tr>
<tr><td></td><td></td><td>Age 75 and over</td><td>4,370</td></tr>
<tr><td>*14,600*
(3,525)</td><td></td><td>Reduced by £1 for every £2 of excess of income over £14,000 to personal relief level (£3,445)</td><td></td></tr>
<tr><td></td><td>Married couple's allowance</td><td>Age under 65</td><td>1,720*</td></tr>
<tr><td></td><td></td><td>Age 65–74</td><td>2,665*</td></tr>
<tr><td></td><td></td><td>Age 75 and over</td><td>2,705*</td></tr>
<tr><td></td><td>Widow's bereavement allowance</td><td>Husband has died during the 2 years to 5 April 1995</td><td>1,720</td></tr>
<tr><td></td><td>Life assurance relief</td><td>Deduction from premiums on policies effected before 14 March 1984</td><td>$12\frac{1}{2}$% of premiums</td></tr>
</table>

Note All of the above reliefs apart from life assurance relief and blind person's allowance will be increased each year in line with the retail price index, unless the Treasury orders otherwise.

15% * Relief restricted to 20% (15% for 1995–6).

2.9 Example: Income Tax Calculation

Tom is married and has income of £35,000 assessable for 1994–5.

On that basis and assuming he does not disclaim the married couple's allowance, his 1994–5 income tax liability is:

Total income		£35,000
Less Personal allowance	3,445	
Married couple's allowance	1,720	5,165
		£29,835

Income tax payable		
At 20%	3,000	600
25%	20,700	5,175
40%	6,135	2,454
	£30,835	£8,229

2.10   Interest and Other Deductions

In arriving at your *total income*, which is taxable after deducting your personal reliefs, certain items are deductible, such as:

Loan interest subject to strict rules.

See 2.12

Business losses and capital allowances. (Previous years' losses are generally only offsettable against income from the same business.)

See 2.19 and 2.18.5

Half of your Class 4 National Insurance contributions.

Certain payments under pre-16 March 1988 court orders for maintenance or alimony.* The relief is restricted to the 1988–9 level.

Annual payments to individuals under deeds of covenant entered into before 15 March 1988.* Relief is restricted to tax at the basic rate only and does not cover payments to your infant children (under age 18).

Donations under deed of covenant to charities; also net donations under the 'Gift Aid Scheme' of at least £250.*

Allowable personal pension contributions, etc.

* These items are examples of *annual payments*, from which you must deduct 25% basic rate income tax on payment. If your income less allowance is insufficient to cover your annual payments, your personal allowances, etc. are restricted.

By deducting tax at the basic rate of 25% from your annual payments and only paying the net amount, you effectively obtain basic rate tax relief. If you are a higher rate tax payer and the annual payment entitles you to relief at the higher rate, your tax liability is reduced accordingly.

2.11 Example: Restriction of Personal Allowances

Suppose your income for 1994–5 is £6,165, your gross annual payments are £2,500, you are married and have the benefit of the married couple's allowance. Your personal allowances will be restricted as follows:

Income		£6,165
Less annual payments		2,500
		3,665
Personal allowance	3,445	
Married couple's allowance	1,720	
	5,165	
Less: restriction	1,500	3,665
		NIL

Note In this example, £1,500 of your allowances is unused. However, if your wife has sufficient income, you could elect for the unused £1,500 to go to her.

2.12   Tax Relief for Interest Payments

If you make interest payments for certain purposes, you deduct it in arriving at your taxable income. In general, this does not apply to bank overdraft or credit card interest. However, interest on business overdrafts is normally deductible in arriving at the business profits.

The following are some examples of loan interest payments for which tax relief is normally obtained:

Interest on loans (including bank overdrafts) used wholly and exclusively for the purposes of a trade, profession or vocation.

Loans to buy your house. Interest on no more than £30,000 attracts relief, at a tax rate which is restricted to 20% (15% after 5 April 1995). If you are over 65 and take a loan to buy a life annuity, the relief rate is 25%. If you have more than one house, only your main residence qualifies for relief.

Other loans to buy properties in the UK. You must let the property for at least 26 weeks in the year at a commercial rent and at other times it needs to be available for letting. The relief is available against the rental income of that or other properties.

Loans to pay inheritance tax.

Purchasing a share in a partnership or lending it money for its business if you are a partner.

Acquiring ordinary shares in a 'close' trading company or lending it money for use in its business. You must either own more than 5% of the share or own some shares and work in the business.

2.13   MIRAS

MIRAS stands for mortgage interest relief at source. Provided your loan qualifies for relief, you deduct tax at 20% from your mortgage interest payments. If your loan exceeds £30,000 you may deduct 20% income tax from the interest on the £30,000 fraction. (After 5 April 1995, the deduction is at 15%.)

Even if your income is less than your personal allowances or you have none at all, you are still allowed the full benefit of MIRAS.

2.14   How Different Types of Income are Taxed

Earlier in this chapter there is a table of the different classes of income. The next pages consider some of the special rules relating to:

See 2.15   Dividends and interest

See 2.16   Land and property

See 2.17   Employment

See 2.18   Businesses and professions

2.15   Dividends and Interest

2.15.1

Dividends are taxed in a special way. Strictly, the company does not deduct tax from your dividends but you receive them with a tax credit of $\frac{20}{80}$ths. This is equivalent to 20% on your gross dividends (including tax credits). If you are a higher rate payer, you are charged 40% on the gross but deduct your 20% tax credit. You thus only pay 20% more.

To the extent that your dividends fall within your basic or lower rate bands, you pay no more income tax. For these purposes, your dividends are taken to be the top slice of your income.

2.15.2 Example: Tax on Dividends

Jill has a taxable income after allowances for 1994–5 of £25,100. This includes dividends of £4,000 with tax credits of £1,000.

Jill's 1994–5 tax liability will be:

General income	£3,000 at 20%	£600
	17,100* at 25%	4,275
Dividends	3,600* at 20%	720
	1,400 at 40%	560
		6,155
Less: tax credits		1,000
Net income tax payable		**£5,155**

* Jill is effectively taxed at 25% on £17,100 of her basic rate band but only 20% on the remaining £3,600.

2.15.3

Bank and building society interest is normally paid to you net of basic rate income tax of 25%. Thus if you receive £75, the gross equivalent is £100. If you pay higher rate tax, this will be £40 and so you will actually pay £15 more.

If you pay no tax, you can elect to receive the interest gross. You need to complete a certificate for each bank, etc., concerned. At the other end of the scale, certain certificates of deposit, etc. for at least £50,000 carry gross interest.

2.15.4

Interest on Government securities is normally paid to you under the deduction of basic rate income tax at 25%. However, certain of these securities

23

can be held for you on the National Savings Stock Register and the interest will then be paid to you gross. You will then be assessed to tax under Schedule D Case III (see below).

Interest is also paid gross on certain Government securities if you are not ordinarily resident here and make the necessary claim to the Revenue.

2.15.5

Interest not taxed at source is normally taxed under *Schedule D Case III*. The basis of assessment is the income that you received in the previous tax year. However, for the opening year and the closing year that you own a source of income, you are assessed on the actual income arising in each year.

If the income first arose later than 6 April, the assessment for the second tax year will also be 'actual'. You have the option to have the third (second) year adjusted to 'actual'. The Revenue have a similar option for the penultimate tax year.

An actual basis of assessment applies for 1996–7 and subsequent years. Thus your 1996–7 assessment will be based on your income for that year. If you acquire a new source of income after 5 April 1994, you will be assessed on the income on an actual basis from the first year onwards.

2.16   Land and Property Income

2.16.1

See 4.5 for 1995–6 simplifications

Schedule A catches most income from land and buildings. An important exception is furnished lettings income. This is assessed under Schedule D Case VI, unless you elect that it should be taxed under Schedule A.

You normally are assessed on the income to which you become entitled in the tax year, less your expenses relating to each property and certain unused losses. The losses may relate to the same or other properties. Allowable expenses include:

Repairs, redecorating and maintenance

Insurance premiums relating to the building

Rents or other periodical payments in respect of the land

Management costs, rent collection, advertising for new tenants, legal and accountancy charges, etc.

Lighting common parts and garden upkeep

Architects' and surveyors' fees regarding maintenance but not improvements

Capital allowances on plant and machinery that you use in the upkeep of the property. If it is an industrial building used for industrial purposes by the tenant, you may get capital allowances on the building. This also applies to some hotels.

See 2.18.5

The tax is payable on 1 January in the tax year. However, at that stage you will not know the profit to the following 5 April. So you first pay on the basis of the figures for the previous year and later pay the balance or receive a refund.

2.16.2 Example: Payment of Schedule A Income Tax

Harry has net Schedule A income for the year to 5 April 1994 of £20,000 and £24,000 for the following year. Assuming that his other income absorbs his personal allowances and basic rate band, his Schedule A liability for 1994–5 will be payable as follows:

1 January 1995 – based on 1993–4 profit	£20,000 at 40%	£8,000
Revised assessment based on 1994–5 profit	£24,000 at 40%	9,600
Additional income tax payable		£1,600

2.16.3

Lease Premiums may be liable to Schedule A income tax. This happens where you get a premium from granting a lease of no more than 50 years on a property that you own. The amount to be taxed under Schedule A is reduced by $\frac{1}{50}$th for each complete period of 12 months (other than the first) that the lease lasts. The remainder generally attracts capital gains tax.

2.16.4

Furnished lettings are normally assessed under Schedule D Case VI, unless you have elected for Schedule A to apply (see above). The basis is the actual income less expenditure for the tax year, including a deduction to cover depreciation on furniture and fittings.

Your deduction may consist of the whole replacement cost each year. However, it is more likely that you will obtain a deduction of 10% of your rents less any rates, etc. and service charges you pay.

Where, under the letting terms, you provide services like meals, domestic help or laundry, you can deduct the costs from your profits.

Losses from furnished letting can be set against other Schedule D Case VI income during the tax year from lettings or miscellaneous income. Any unrelieved losses are carried forward and set against future Schedule D Case VI assessments.

2.16.5

Rent a room is a scheme which provides relief where you rent furnished accommodation in your only or main home. If your rents from this source are no more than £3,250 in any tax year, they are completely exempted from tax.

If your rent is more than £3,250, you have the option of paying tax on the excess, with no allowance for expenses. Alternatively, you pay on the conventional basis. You need to elect for the alternative basis within one year of the end of the tax year to which it applies.

2.16.6 Example: Rent a Room

Joy, who is a basic rate tax payer, rents a room in her house and receives £4,250 for 1994–5. Her allowable expenses are £2,050.

If Joy elects for the alternative basis, she will be assessed for 1994–5 on £4,250–3,250 = £1,000.
Tax at 25% is £250.

With no election, the assessment is £4,250–2,050 = £2,200.
Tax at 25% is £550.

Thus Joy clearly should make the election, thereby saving £300.

2.16.7

Furnished holiday lettings may attract certain reliefs which are only normally available for trades for tax purposes. In order to do so, the accommodation must be available for holiday letting for at least 140 days each tax year. It must actually be let for at least 70 days in the year and no let normally is to exceed 31 days.

The reliefs obtained include capital gains tax roll-over relief and retirement relief. Also loss relief as for trades, capital allowances and personal pensions relief.

2.17 Employment Income

Your income from any employment, including directorships, is normally taxed under Schedule E. This usually means Pay As You Earn (PAYE). Under the PAYE system, your employer deducts tax and National Insurance contributions from your salary. A receipts basis is followed, so that you are taxed on the basis of what you are paid.

27

2.17.1

Amounts included in your taxable income include:

Normal salary and overtime pay
Salary in lieu of notice, though often tax free
Sick pay including statutory sick pay
Sickness insurance benefits
Luncheon vouchers in excess of 15 pence each day
Director's fees and other remuneration
Payment for entering into contract of employment
Value of goods supplied free to you by your employer
Unapproved pension scheme contributions
Share options
Maternity pay
Tips from employer or customers
Christmas or other annual gifts (except some personal ones)
Bonuses and commission
Fringe benefits (see below).

2.17.2

Expenses may be claimed by you provided that they are incurred wholly, exclusively and necessarily in performing the duties of your employment. Excluded is your travel between home and work and generally entertaining. Typical items are:

Travelling
Business use of your own car
Home telephone and other expenses
Overalls, other work clothing and tools
Professional fees and subscriptions
Your own contributions to an approved pension scheme run by your
 employers
In certain employments, special deductions may apply; for example in
 the entertainment industry, hairdressing, make-up, clothes cleaning,
 etc.

2.17.3

Fringe benefits is a term used for any tangible benefit from your employment not included in your pay cheque. The taxation of your fringe benefits depends upon whether you earn less than £8,500 annually. In that case, it is less stringent.

Otherwise, a more severe basis applies, also normally used for directors. Your employers must then submit to the Revenue form P11D each year covering your benefits and expenses. The £8,500 earnings limit was set many years ago, when many employees fell below this, but is of much less importance today. The following table only covers P11D employees.

2.17.4 Fringe Benefits – Tax Treatment

Details	Tax treatment
Travelling and entertainment	See 2.17.5
Motor car provided by employers	Taxable based on list price when bought – see 2.17.6
Motor van provided for you	Taxable amount of £500 (£350 if at least 4 years old)
Rent-free company house	Taxed on its annual value unless you must live there to do your job
Board and lodging	Taxed on cost to employer, subject to a limit of 10% of your net emoluments
Share options	Taxable
Employees' outings	Normally tax free
Subsidised staff canteens	Tax free if available for all staff
Luncheon vouchers	First 15p per day is tax free
Working clothing, eg overalls	Tax free
Suits, coats etc.	Taxed on cost to employers
Private sickness insurance	Taxed on premiums paid by employer
Interest-free loan	Taxable subject to certain exemptions
Season tickets and credit cards	Normally taxable
Cash vouchers	Taxable
Pension and death in service cover	Normally tax free
Assets placed at your disposal	Normally taxable at 20% of the value when first obtained
Scholarships for your children	Taxable with some exceptions
Long service awards (20 years)	Articles or employer company shares (up to £20 each year) are tax free
Mobile telephones privately used	Taxed on £200 each year
Childcare	Tax free subject to some conditions
Removal expenses and benefits	Up to £8,000 normally tax free

2.17.5

Travelling and entertainment allowances or advances paid to you by your employer are not normally taxable. Of course, you need to spend the money for these purposes on your employer's behalf. Your employer obtains relief for payments to you for your travelling expenses, but not normally entertaining. Your expenses of travelling to and from work are not allowable.

The cost of your travelling abroad in connection with your employer's business is deductible. Furthermore, if you work abroad for at least 60 continuous days, you can pay for your family to visit you. You will have no taxable benefit on the fares. There is a limit of two return trips each tax year for your spouse and each child under 18 years old.

2.17.6

Motor cars provided by employers give rise to benefit charges based on the list prices of the vehicles. To this is added the price of any extras provided. You are then taxed on 35% of this, subject to a one-third discount if your annual business mileage exceeds 2,500. If this is more than 18,000 the discount is two-thirds.

If you have two cars provided, your benefit for the 'second car' is only discounted if your annual business mileage exceeds 18,000; and then by one-third only. With vintage cars over 15 years old, whose market values are over £15,000, your benefit is based on market value.

Where your car is at least four years old at the end of the tax year, your discounted benefit is reduced by one-third. One consolation, if your list price exceeds £80,000, your benefit will be calculated using this figure.

The provision of petrol or diesel fuel for you by your employer gives rise to a separate benefit charge. This depends on the engine size of your car and whether it runs on petrol or diesel, as is shown by the following table.

(1995–6) **2.17.7 Car Fuel Benefits 1994–5**

Cylinder capacity	Petrol (£)		Diesel (£)
1400cc or less	640	(670)	580 (605)
1401–2000cc	810	(850)	580 (605)
Over 2000cc	1,200	(1,260)	750 (780)

The tax rules relating to employment take in many areas, which are outside the scope of this chapter. Examples are share option and incentive schemes, profit-sharing schemes, retirement pension arrangements and compensation for loss of office. However, where relevant to later sections of the book, explanations appear subsequently.

See 8.4.4 etc
See 8.2 etc

2.18   Business and Professional Income

Your profits from a trade are normally assessed under Schedule D Case I. Trade includes manufacturing, wholesaling, retailing and all sorts of trading ventures.

Professions and vocations are covered by Schedule D Case II. A profession is broadly an occupation needing special intellectual and sometimes manual skills. Examples are medicine, law and accountancy. A vocation is in essence the way that a person passes his or her life, such as a writer, actor or musician.

2.18.1

Assessable profits are computed from your annual profit and loss account or income and expenditure account. These should be drawn up to the same date each year but need not coincide with the tax year and end on 5 April. (If your annual turnover is less than £15,000, you simply complete three lines in your tax return giving your sales, deductions and net profit.)

Your accounts profit normally requires adjusting for tax purposes in some of the following ways:

● Add to your profit (or deduct from your loss) any non-deductible expenses charged in the accounts, including:

Items not laid out wholly and exclusively for the business
Private expenses
Capital expenditure, such as building improvements and plant
Reserves and provisions for anticipated expenses, including general bad debt reserves but not reserves for specific bad debts
Losses not connected with the business
Payments of income tax, capital gains tax, etc.
Your own drawings
Depreciation and amortisation of plant and machinery, buildings, etc.
Entertaining expenses unless in connection with your own staff
Annuities or other annual payments (not interest) from which you deduct income tax.

● Add to your profit any items that are not taxed under Schedule D Cases I & II. This could either be because they are not taxable or because they are taxable under another Case or Schedule. Examples are capital profits and interest.

● Deduct from your profits any expenses not charged in your accounts which are nevertheless allowable for tax.

● Add to your profits any trading profits not already included.

● From your profits computed as above, deduct your capital allowances for the year.

2.18.2

The basis of assessment under Schedule D Cases I & II is normally the profits earned in the accounts year ending in the preceding tax year. Thus, if your business makes up its accounts to 30 June, its assessment for 1995–6 will be based on the profits for the year to 30 June 1994. Special rules apply for the opening and closing years.

*See
2.18.3*

A new system operates from 1996–7. For that year, the assessment will be based on the average of the profits for the two years ending in 1996–7. After that, the assessment for any tax year will be based on the accounts ending in that tax year. No special basis for opening and closing years will then be necessary.

If your business starts after 5 April 1994, the new assessment basis applies throughout. Suppose you commence trading on 1 July 1994 and 30 June is to be your regular accounting date. Your 1994–5 assessment will be based on your profits from 1 July 1994 to 5 April 1995 and that for 1995–6 on the profits for the year to 30 June 1995.

2.18.3

The special assessment rules for the opening and closing years under the present rules for existing businesses are:

The assessment for the first year is based on the profits from the starting date until the next 5 April. If necessary, you apportion your profits if your accounts do not cover that period.

The assessment for the second year is normally based on the profits for the first 12 months of trading.

The assessment for the third year is normally on the preceding basis (the profits for the accounts ending in the preceding tax year). However, you can elect for the second and third years together to be assessed on actual.

Where there is a permanent cessation, the assessment for the last tax year is based on the profits from 6 April until the date when trading stopped.

The Revenue may increase the assessments already made for the two years prior to the tax year when trading stopped. The adjustment is to increase those assessments to the actual profits for the two years prior to the last.

2.18.4 Example: Assessment Under Schedule D Cases I & II

Harry started in business on 1 July 1992 and prepared accounts for 18 months to 31 December 1993 and annually thereafter. His adjusted profits are:

18 months to 31 December 1993	£27,000
Year 1994	3,600
.... 1995	7,200
.... 1996	20,000
.... 1997	30,000

The profits for the second and third years are much down on the first. Therefore Harry will make a good saving by electing for them to be assessed on an actual basis. His assessments will then be:

Tax year	Base period	Calculation		Assessment
1992–3	1.7.92–5.4.93	$£27,000 \times \dfrac{9\frac{1}{6}}{18}$		£13,750
1993–4	6.4.93–31.12.93	$£27,000 \times \dfrac{8\frac{5}{6}}{18}$	£13,250	
	1.1.94–5.4.94	$£3,600 \times \dfrac{3\frac{1}{6}}{12}$	£950	£14,200
1994–5	6.4.94–31.12.94	$£3,600 \times \dfrac{8\frac{5}{6}}{12}$	£2,650	
	1.1.95–5.4.95	$£7,200 \times \dfrac{3\frac{1}{6}}{12}$	£1,900	£4,550
1995–6	1.1.94–31.12.94			£3,600
1996–7	Average of 1995 & 1996	$\dfrac{£27,200}{2}$		£13,600
1997–8	1.1.97–31.12.97			£30,000

2.18.5

Capital allowances are available on a wide range of assets, including the following categories at the rates shown:

See
2.18.6

Plant and machinery including furniture, fittings, office equipment and motor cars, 25% writing down allowance (WDA)

Industrial buildings including factories, etc., 4% straight line WDA

Agricultural and forestry buildings, 4% straight line WDA

Hotel buildings, 4% straight line WDA

Scientific research expenditure, 100% of capital costs, excluding some items such as land and houses

Patents and know-how, 25% WDA

Mines and oilwells, 10 or 25% WDA

Dredging, 4% straight line WDA

Note Unless otherwise indicated, WDAs are computed on the reducing balance, after deducting previous allowances.

2.18.6

Capital allowances on plant and machinery are calculated on a 'pool' basis. Each asset that you buy is put into your pool of assets. Writing down allowance is then calculated at 25% on and deducted from the pool balance. If you wish, you can elect for a lower rate of allowance or none at all to apply for a given year. Where assets are sold from your pool, the proceeds are deducted.

Special rules apply to motor cars costing more than £12,000. Each is put into a separate pool and the writing down allowance is limited to £3,000. As soon as the balance falls below £12,000, the allowance reverts to 25%.

Short-life assets may also be treated as being outside your pool, provided you make the necessary election. When you sell the assets, there will be a balancing allowance or charge (taxable), depending on whether there is a deficit or surplus. Where it has not been sold within five years, it must be transferred to your pool at its tax written down value.

2.18.7

Enterprise zones, which are specially designated by the Government, have many attractions, including special capital allowance rules. In particular, a 100% initial allowance is available in the first year on industrial and commercial buildings. These include shops, offices and hotels. You can claim less than 100%. In that case, 25% writing down allowance is given on the cost on a straight line basis, until used up.

2.19   Business Loss Relief

Relief for losses in your business is available according to the rules. You augment your adjusted trading loss by your capital allowances and, on making a claim, obtain relief. This is first given against your other income for the tax year in which you suffer the loss. Any balance then goes against income for the next tax year. You can also elect for any unused balance to be set against your capital gains.

Special rules apply for new businesses (and for terminal losses not considered here). The relief covers any loss in your first tax year or any of the next three, including capital allowances. You obtain relief against your income for the three years of assessment prior to the year in which the losses are made, taking the earliest first.

The above relief normally needs to be claimed within two years of the end of the tax year to which it relates. Any losses not dealt with as above are normally carried forward to be set against future profits from the same trade only.

The loss rules are changing from 1997–8 for businesses existing at 5 April 1994 and from commencement if after that date. Losses will be computed on the basis of the periods for which the accounts are prepared, instead of the present fiscal year basis. You may allocate the losses against your other income for the year of loss or the previous year.

2.20   Partnerships

Trades and professions are often carried out in partnership. For tax purposes, a joint assessment is made on the partners in respect of the partnership profits. This includes the lower, basic and higher tax rates. The normal capital allowance rules are followed as are those for the opening and closing years.

The joint assessment is split between the partners according to their profit-sharing ratios during the tax year. (These ratios may not be the same as for the year when the profits were earned.) Interest and salaries are normally treated as Schedule D earnings for profit-sharing partners.

Partnership losses are divided between the partners in their profit-sharing ratios. Each can then use them as he or she pleases. Capital gains are split in the ratio that the partners share in the assets.

Where there is a change in the composition of the partnership, this is treated as a cessation. However, an election can be made within two years of the change, signed by all of the old and new partners, for a continuation basis to apply.

Where the change is treated as a cessation, special rules apply for the new partnership. The first four years are assessed on an actual basis and then the previous year basis applies. However, you can elect for the 'actual' basis also to apply for years five and six.

New rules apply for partnerships commencing after 5 April 1994 and generally from 1997–8. Partners will be assessed individually on the basis of periods of account and from 1996–7 self-assessment will apply.

2.21   Domicile and Residence

Your tax liability is much affected by your domicile and residence. Only individuals have domiciles. However, companies, settlements and partnerships have residences, as well as individuals.

2.21.1

Your *domicile* is the country which you consider as your natural home. Generally, it would be your country of birth. Under English law you can only have one domicile at any time, although this may later change. Your domicile is likely to fall within three main categories:

Domicile of origin
Domicile of choice
Domicile of dependency

2.21.2

Your *residence* is fixed by your circumstances from year to year. Furthermore, for tax purposes, you may be regarded as being resident in two or more countries at once. Depending on the facts, your residence will be determined by:

Your presence in a country
Your objects in being in the country
The time spent in the country during the tax year
Your future intentions regarding length of stay
Whether you have a place of abode here (now of less importance than
    before)
If you visit the UK temporarily, you are normally treated as resident if
    you spend 183 days or more here
Habitual substantial visits may cause you to be regarded as UK resident.
    This would apply if you average 90 days or more each tax year over a
    four-year period.

2.21.3

Ordinary residence is a more permanent type of residence, and is not casual nor uncertain. It implies that it is the country where you live in the ordinary course of your life.

2.22 The Effect of Domicile and Residence on Your Tax

The following table illustrates the incidence of income tax, capital gains tax and inheritance tax, depending on where you are domiciled and resident.

Tax	Where income arises/ situation of assets	Tax treatment		
		Arising basis	Remittance basis	Tax free
Income tax				
Schedule D				
Cases I & II	UK	All classes		
	Abroad	n/a		
Case III	UK	Normally all classes		
	Abroad	n/a		
Cases IV & V apart from trades, professions, pensions, etc.	UK	n/a	n/a	
	Abroad	UKD	ND UKD but NOR	NR
		R & OR		
Case V re trades, professions, pensions, etc.	UK	n/a	n/a	
	Abroad	UKD R & OR	ND UKD R but NOR	NR
		(90% pensions)		
Case VI	UK	All classes		
	Abroad	n/a apart from certain anti-avoidance rules		
Schedule E	(see 2.17)			
Capital gains tax	UK or Abroad	UKD & R/OR	ND but R/OR (UK assets on arising basis)	NR & NOR

		Tax treatment		
Tax	**Where income arises/ situation of assets**	**Arising basis**	**Remittance basis**	**Tax free**
Inheritance tax (residence normally immaterial)	UK	UKD/ND		ND
	Abroad	UKD/deemed domiciled		

Key	UKD	United Kingdom domiciled
	ND	Non-United Kingdom domiciled
	R	United Kingdom resident
	OR	Ordinarily resident in UK
	NOR	Not ordinarily resident in UK
	NR	Not resident in UK

2.23   Anti-Avoidance Legislation

As previously mentioned, tax avoidance is perfectly legal. However, much legislation has been enacted to counter it. This often results in taxation, particularly under Schedule D Case VI.

In some cases, advance clearance can be obtained from the Inland Revenue. You submit full particulars of proposed transactions to them and they notify you as to whether specific anti-avoidance legislation applies. This procedure is particularly useful concerning company reorganisations and takeovers.

The following are some examples of anti-avoidance provisions, giving references to the 1988 Taxes Act:

Transactions in securities resulting in a tax advantage (Ss703–709)

Transfer of assets abroad where a UK ordinarily resident person has power to enjoy the income (Ss739–746)

Sales at under- or overvalue between connected persons including companies (Ss770–774)

Sale of income from personal activities for capital (S775)

Artificial transactions in land producing capital profits (Ss776–777)

Schemes where interest is 'manufactured' (S787)

Controlled foreign companies with low tax rates (Ss747–756)

Company migration (S765)

Capital gains tax provisions include: non-resident trusts, sales of subsidiaries, 'value-shifting', company takeovers and reconstructions and offshore funds.

2.24 Corporation Tax

The tax on the profits and capital gains of a company is called corporation tax. The following paragraphs give just a few pointers on what is a very complex subject.

Corporation tax is charged on an actual basis on the total for each accounting period of income under the various Schedules and Cases and capital gains. Capital allowances are computed and deducted, as are losses. Accounting periods usually coincide with those for which annual accounts are prepared. However, they cannot exceed 12 months.

The full corporation tax rate is 33%. However, a 25% small companies rate applies if the profits for the year do not exceed £300,000. If they are between £300,000 and £1,500,000 there is some 'marginal relief'. The tax is broadly 33% on the profits, less $\frac{1}{50}$th of the amount by which they fall short of £1,500,000.

If your company has 'associated companies', the figures £300,000 and £1,500,000 mentioned above are reduced. They are each divided by the number of 'associated companies' plus one, for small companies rate purposes. 'Associated companies' are broadly those under common control or where one controls the other. Control can involve voting power or the right to more than half of the profits or of the assets on liquidation.

2.25   Advance Corporation Tax

Advance corporation tax (ACT) is paid by companies on their dividends, etc. The rate is $\frac{20}{80}$ths of the dividend payments. The ACT is accounted for to the Revenue on a quarterly basis. These payments are treated as advance payments of so called 'mainstream corporation tax' and are set against the final amount due. Any unrelieved ACT can be carried back up to six years and carried forward indefinitely.

2.26   Groups

Groups of companies often receive special reliefs. Broadly the effect is to treat them in certain respects as if they were one company.

A group is broadly a parent and subsidiaries. A 51% subsidiary is owned as to more than 50% by its parent and a 75% subsidiary is not less than 75% so owned. The following are examples of available reliefs within groups:

Group loss relief for parent and 75% subsidiaries

Inter-group (51%) dividend and interest payments without ACT or income tax deduction

Transfers of assets within a group consisting of parent and 75% subsidiaries are normally capital gains tax free

Transfers of ACT relief from parent to 51% subsidiaries

Capital gains tax roll-over relief within a group consisting of parent and 75% subsidiaries. Capital gains on assets sold by one company 'rolled-over' into purchases of assets by others.

CHAPTER THREE

Capital Taxes –
Some Basic Rules

3.1 Introduction

See Appendix 13–14 This chapter deals with capital taxes and in particular capital gains tax and inheritance tax. Stamp duty is not covered here, since it is of only relatively modest impact. However, rates are given at the end of the book.

Both capital gains tax and inheritance tax are highly important areas for tax planning. There are many opportunities built in to the system, as are later described. But first it helps to know some basic rules.

3.2 Capital Gains Tax

This tax is payable on your capital gains during each tax year. (Husband and wife are taxed separately.) There are various reliefs as later described and you deduct your capital losses. There is an annual exemption of *1995–6 £6,000 (£3,000)* £5,800 (broadly £2,900 for trusts). Your tax is charged at the same rates as income tax. However, the capital gains tax rules are quite different.

The tax is payable on 1 December following the tax year or, if later, 30 days after the issue of the assessment. However, regarding certain gifts and cases of hardship, you are allowed to pay by instalments.

3.3   Who is Liable?

Companies, trusts, partnerships and individuals are all liable to capital gains tax. However, you have to be resident and/or ordinarily resident here. If you are non-domiciled, you are only liable on your overseas capital gains to the extent that you remit these to the UK. *For definitions see 2.21*

You may still be taxed even though you are neither resident nor ordinarily resident. If you carry on a trade here through a branch or agency, you will normally be liable on UK disposals of assets related to your trade, etc.

3.4   The Tax Rates on Capital Gains

● Individuals pay capital gains tax at 20%, 25% and 40%.

● Companies pay corporation tax on their capital gains at their appropriate rates (25% or 33% etc).

● Accumulation and maintenance trusts and discretionary settlements have a 35% rate. Other trusts normally pay at 25%. (An exception is where the settlor or spouse has any interest or rights in the settlement, when his or her rates apply.)

To calculate the rates that you pay, take your total gains less losses for the tax year and deduct your capital losses brought forward. You then deduct your annual exemption (£5,800). Also some unrelieved trading losses may be offsettable. *(1995–6 £6,000)*

The balance of your gains together with your taxable income after allowances are then considered. For 1994–5, £3,000 is taxed at 20%, £20,700 at 25% and the remainder at 40%. Your income is taxed first at your lower rates and your capital gains thus attract your higher rates. *1995–6 rates see 4.2*

3.5 Example: Tax on Capital Gains

Emma has income after allowances for 1994–5 of £18,700 and net capital gains (after losses) of £15,800. Her capital gains tax is:

Upper limit of 25% band		£23,700
Less income after allowances		18,700
Unused balance of 25% band		£5,000
Net capital gains		£15,800
Less annual exemption		5,800
Taxable balance		£10,000
Capital gains tax payable	£5,000 at 25%	1,250
	£5,000 at 40%	2,000
		£3,250

3.6   Annual Exemptions for 1994–5

1995–6
£6,000
£5,800 of your net gains is exempted from capital gains tax, no matter how high your total gains. All losses for the tax year must be offset in arriving at the net gains. However, any set-off of losses from previous years is restricted, so as to leave £5,800 of gains to be exempted. This leaves more losses to carry forward.

1995–6
£6,000
The same rules apply for personal representatives (executors, etc.) for the tax year of death and the following two. Trusts for the mentally disabled and those getting attendance allowance also obtain the £5,800 exemption.

1995–6
£3,000
For other trusts, such as accumulation and maintenance or discretionary ones, the annual exemption is £2,900. However, this is divided by the number of trusts set up after 6 June 1978 by the same settlor. Thus if you

46

have set up two such trusts, the exemption for each is thus £1,450. *1995–6*
However, the minimum exemption is set at £580. *£600*

3.7   Assets Liable and Exempted

All forms of property are within the capital gains tax net, subject to certain exemptions. Assets liable include:

Investments including shares, etc.
Land and buildings
Jewellery, pictures, antiques
Currency other than sterling
Property which you create before disposing of it
Options, debts, etc.

3.8   Assets Exempted From Capital Gains Tax

Your main private residence *See*
Foreign currency for personal expenditure abroad *3.21.3*
Betting winnings, e.g. pools, premium bonds, etc.
British Government securities and certain corporate bonds
Life assurance policies and deferred annuities where you are the first
   owner or they were gifted to you
Chattels sold for no more than £6,000 *See*
Private motor vehicles *3.21.1*
Gifts of assets of national, scientific or historic interest and land, etc. to
   the National Trust
Gifts of business property, etc. covered by an election *See*
Timber and uncut trees *3.21.7*
BES shares issued to you after 18 March 1986, provided you are the first
   holder
Debts (not 'debts on security'), providing you are the original creditor
Futures and options in gilts and qualifying corporate bonds
Compensation/damages for any wrong or injury suffered to your person
   or concerning your profession or vocation
Assets such as boats, animals, etc., which are both tangible movable
   property and wasting assets (expected life no more than 50 years).
   Land and buildings and assets qualifying for capital allowances are
   not covered.

3.9   What are Disposals for Capital Gains Tax Purposes?

In order for you to be liable to capital gains tax, you need to dispose of an asset in whole or part. The following are examples:

The sale of the whole or part of an asset

The destruction of an asset, such as by fire

The surrender or forfeiture of a right, such as to renew a lease

The sale of a right related to an asset, e.g. a lease out of your freehold

Gifts of assets are treated as disposals at market value although it is sometimes possible to hold over the gains until the assets are sold

The assets which pass on your death are treated as disposals at their market values, free of capital gains tax. Your heirs are treated as acquiring the assets at those values.

Note that if you sell or gift an asset to your spouse, this is not normally treated as a capital gains tax disposal. However, he or she must be living with you during the tax year. What happens is that your spouse's capital gains tax on disposal is computed using your original cost and aquisition date.

Certain other asset transfers are not disposals for capital gains tax purposes. Examples are where you mortgage your house, transfer an asset to a nominee acting on your behalf and gifts of assets to charities.

3.10   Computing Your Chargeable Gains

● For each of your disposals in the tax year, find the consideration. This is usually the sales proceeds. However, open-market value applies for disposals not at arm's length. It also applies for transfers to persons connected with you, such as close relatives (excluding your wife).

● Deduct the cost of each asset (sometimes value at acquisition) and incidental expenses concerning your acquisition and disposal. These include the fees of surveyors, valuers, solicitors, accountants, stamp duty and commission. You also include improvement costs.

See 3.11   ● If you held an asset at 31 March 1982, you substitute its value at that date for the cost, if it gives a better result. This is known as 're-basing'.

- Deduct indexation allowance based on the acquisition costs or 31 March 1982 value and also improvements. *See 3.13*

- Special rules apply for assets held since before 7 April 1965 and for leases and other wasting assets. *See 3.16 and 3.18*

3.11   Re-basing

In theory, the effect of re-basing and indexation is that you only pay capital gains tax when your gains outstrip inflation. Re-Basing is likely to take effect where you sell an asset which you owned on 31 March 1982. Provided it exceeds the cost, the asset's value at 31 March 1982 is automatically taken as its base value at that date.

Re-basing may also apply where you received an asset after 31 March 1982 from someone who held it on that date. This includes where the transfer to you was treated as producing neither gain nor loss. An example is where one spouse acquires an asset from the other.

You cannot normally increase a gain or loss by re-basing. Moreover, where a loss is converted to a gain or vice versa through re-basing, the disposal is treated as resulting in no gain and no loss.

However, you can elect that all of your assets are re-based to their values at 31 March 1982. This is subject to a time limit of two years after the end of the tax year when you made your first disposal after 1987–8.

3.12 Example: Re-Basing

John sells for £2,000 an asset which cost £1,200 and was worth £3,000 on 31 March 1982. Ignoring indexation, his capital gain/loss with and without re-basing is:

With re-basing		
	Proceeds	£2,000
	Value at 31 March 1982	3,000
	LOSS	£1,000

Without re-basing		
	Proceeds	£2,000
	Cost	1,200
	GAIN	£800

John is treated as having no gain and no loss, because with re-basing, he has a loss of £1,000 and without it, a gain of £800.

3.13   Indexation Relief

The effect of indexation relief is to scale up the base cost of your assets in line with inflation. This is done by using the monthly figures of the Retail Price Index starting from March 1982. (The values are shown at the end of this book.)

See Appendix 8

Indexation relief is calculated from the month of acquisition to that of disposal. However, for assets owned at 31 March 1982, it runs from March 1982 until the month of disposal.

For disposals before 30 November 1993 you obtained full indexation relief, even if it created a loss or made one bigger. Subsequently, indexation neither creates nor increases a capital loss.

Where you take over an asset from your spouse, there is no capital gains tax at that time. Your acquisition cost is deemed to be that of your spouse, including indexation up to the date of transfer. When you dispose of the asset, your indexation relief is taken from the date of transfer, on your deemed acquisition cost.

3.14 Example: Indexation Relief

Debbie sells shares on 25 June 1993 for £10,000. They had all been bought on 16 May 1989, when the cost had been £4,000. The Retail Price Indices in the months of purchase and sale were:

May 1989 101.9
June 1993 141.0

Debbie's chargeable gain is:

Proceeds		£10,000
Less cost	£4,000	
Indexation £4,000 × (141 – 100)/101.9	1,535	5,535
		£4,465

3.15   Losses

Various types of losses need to be considered. There are *capital losses*, which are produced when your base value and indexation exceed your proceeds. However, for disposals after 29 November 1993, indexation no longer creates nor increases a capital loss (subject to limited transitional relief).

Apart from the above indexation relief restriction, capital losses are computed in broadly the same way as your chargeable gains. Your capital losses are then deductible from your capital gains for the same tax year. Any surplus is carried forward to set off against gains in future years.

Loss relief does not eat into your annual exemption (£5,800). Thus, suppose your gains for a tax year are £8,800 and your losses £5,000. Only £3,000 will be offset, leaving net gains of £5,800, which are covered by the exemption. Losses of £2,000 are then carried forward.

1995–6 £6,000

Trading losses can be offset against capital gains in some circumstances. This happens if you make a loss in your trade, profession or vocation and have insufficient income to cover it for that tax year. You can then elect to set your unused trading losses against capital gains for that year. Any trading losses still unused can be carried forward to the next tax year and offset first against income and then capital gains.

You can elect to obtain income tax relief for *losses on unquoted shares in trading companies*, subject to the rules. The relief applies where you were an original subscriber in a 'qualifying trading company'. Trading for this purpose excludes dealing mainly in shares, land, etc.

3.16   Assets Owned on 6 April 1965

The present system of capital gains tax only operates for disposals after 6 April 1965. So there are rules to relieve such parts of your gains as relate to earlier years. However, re-basing as at 31 March 1982 has made the earlier rules much less important. The old rules are still used if they produce a better result, unless you have elected for a 31 March 1982 valuation for all your assets.

The general rule is known as the *time apportionment* method. You are relieved from tax on the pre-6 April 1965 proportion of the gain, on the basis that your asset's worth grew uniformly. Thus, if your total gain is G and you held an asset for A months prior to 6 April 1965 and B months from that date until disposal, your taxable gain is $G \times B/(A + B)$.

Note that for time apportionment purposes, you can go back no earlier than 6 April 1945. Another rule is that where indexation relief is available, you must apply this before time apportionment. This reduces the benefit of indexation.

Time apportionment does not apply to quoted shares. Instead, relief is given with reference to the 6 April 1965 value. (There is also an election, now broadly out of time, for all your quoted shares to be valued at that date.) However, re-basing at 31 March 1982 normally produces a higher value.

For other assets qualifying in time apportionment, valuation at 6 April

1965 exists as an option. An election is needed, within two years of the end of the tax year of sale. This is seldom now made, because 31 March 1982 re-basing is normally better.

3.17   Part Disposals

If you dispose of part of an asset, you need to compute the cost attributable to the part sold. You do this by multiplying the original cost by $A/(A+B)$. A is the proceeds from the part sold and B is the value of the remainder at that date of the part disposal. You then calculate indexation (if applicable). Where it is more, the value at 31 March 1982 is used instead of the cost.

Part disposals of land have special treatment, provided the proceeds do not exceed £20,000 during the tax year, or one-fifth of its total value. You have the option of deducting the proceeds from the base cost, rather than paying tax now.

3.18   Leases And Other Wasting Assets

'Wasting assets' have a predictable life of no more than 50 years and exclude freehold land and buildings. Wasting assets which are also movable property (chattels) are usually not liable to capital gains tax.

For other wasting assets, apart from leases, you must reduce the original costs on a straight line basis over their lives. Thus, if you buy a wasting asset with 20 years to run for £8,000 and sell it 10 years later, your allowable cost is 10/20ths = £4,000.

A special formula applies for writing off leases of land and buildings with no more than 50 years to run. The rate of wastage accelerates as the lease runs its course. If you sell such a lease and lease back your premises for less than 15 years, income tax may be charged on a proportion of the proceeds.

3.19   Quoted Shares

A pooling basis applies to all of the quoted shares that you hold of the same class in the same company. You have one 'pool' for shares acquired after 5 April 1982 and one for earlier acquisitions. 'Pooling' does not apply to your 6 April 1965 holdings, unless there is an election for them all to be valued at that date.

A 'pool' is indistinguishable from its constituent parts. Thus, suppose your purchases of shares in A Ltd were:

Date	Number of shares	Cost £
4 June 1985	1,000	5,000
6 September 1987	2,000	8,000
7 December 1990	1,000	7,000
	4,000	20,000

If you sell 1,000 shares in May 1995, they are not treated as being the original ones which you bought. They are regarded as coming from your 'pool' at the average cost price, which is £20,000/4,000 = £5 per share.

3.19.1

Identification and indexation are both involved when you sell quoted shares from an active pool. The following are some guidelines regarding sales after 5 April 1985, before which different rules applied.

Shares which you sell are first identified with your post-5 April 1982 pool, then your pre-6 April 1982 pool and finally your unpooled 6 April 1965 holdings. Where beneficial, re-basing at 31 March 1982 will apply.

Indexation must be calculated separately on the different parts. The pre-6 April 1982 'pool' should present no problem, normally being re-based.

The post-5 April 1982 'pool' must be looked at carefully. Each additional purchase carries indexation from the purchase date. Thus, indexation relief is added to the pool before each purchase and sale. For each sale, the total cost and relief is the proportion attributable to the shares sold.

3.19.2

Bonus issues and takeovers are subject to special rules. For example, you may receive a bonus issue of shares of the same class as your existing holding. You must then treat the new shares as having been acquired when your original shares were bought.

Thus, suppose you bought 2,000 shares in B Ltd at £3 each in 1986 and now obtain a bonus of one share for every two that you hold. You will be treated as having acquired 3,000 shares in 1986 at a cost of £2 each.

'Rights' to subscribe for additional shares are similarly treated. If you take them up, your new shares are regarded as having been purchased at the same time as your existing ones. If you sell the 'rights' without taking up the shares, this is a part disposal.

Takeovers are treated as normal disposals, to the extent that you receive cash. If the consideration consists of shares and/or debentures, your capital gains tax is normally deferred until you sell your new 'paper'. There are certain conditions and anti-avoidance rules. In particular, one company needs to own or obtain through the takeover over 25% of the ordinary shares of the other.

3.20 Unquoted Shares

Although many of the above points hold good, different rules sometimes apply for unquoted shares, as opposed to quoted ones. For example, time apportionment is available for 6 April 1965 holdings, together with individual rather than blanket valuation elections.

In practice, various reliefs are obtainable regarding shares in unquoted rather than quoted companies. These include roll-over relief on rein-vestment, gifts relief and retirement relief. Fuller details appear below.

3.21 Special Reliefs

There are various special reliefs for capital gains tax purposes, which are important for tax-planning purposes. These are summarised below and where appropriate, covered in more detail later.

3.21.1

Chattels sold for £6,000 or less are free of capital gains tax. If your proceeds exceed £6,000, your capital gain is restricted to five-thirds of the excess. An asset is a chattel if it is tangible movable property, for example a picture or a table. furthermore, a set is treated as one chattel.

3.21.2

Charities are exempted from capital gains tax on gains from the disposal of any assets, provided the gains are applied to charitable purposes. Where you gift an asset to a charity, you pay no capital gains tax on this disposal.

3.21.3

Your *main residence* (including land of half a hectare) is normally exempt from capital gains tax when you sell it. However, your relief may be restricted if you lived elsewhere or rented out your house, etc. If part is rented out, your relief on that part is restricted to the exemption on the part you occupy, or £40,000 if less.

Your exemption is not lost if since 31 March 1982, your absences from the house keep within the following aggregated limits:

The last 36 months of ownership
Periods of absence totalling three years
Any periods worked abroad
Any periods up to a total of four years when the location of your
    employment prevents you from living in your house
Periods in job-related accommodation whilst intending to return to
    your main residence.

If a specific part of your house is set aside for business purposes, this part does not qualify for relief. However, if no room is exclusively used for business, you will not generally lose any relief. This applies even though you claim a fraction of your house expenses against your business profits.

Where you have two residences, you may elect as to which is your main residence and thus eligible for relief. The election must be made within two years of your second acquisition. Failing this, the Revenue will decide as to which is your main residence on the basis of the facts, such as the time you spend in each.

3.21.4

Roll-over relief is the popular name for the relief available on the replacement of certain business assets. Where such assets are sold and others purchased within one year before and three years after the sale, 'roll-over' relief applies. The gain on the disposal is deducted from the cost of the new asset so that no capital gains tax is payable until its sale.

In order to obtain the relief, both the old and new assets must belong to one or another of various qualifying classes. These include land and buildings, fixed plant and machinery not being part of a building, ships, aircraft and hovercraft, and goodwill. Since, to qualify, plant and machinery must be fixed, items such as motor vans are excluded.

To obtain total relief, the entire proceeds must be reinvested. Failing this, you pay capital gains tax in respect of the shortfall. The old and new assets must be used in the same business. However, if you have several trades, they count as one for this purpose. Purchases and sales by you of assets used in your 'family company' also qualify for the relief.

3.21.5

Roll-over relief on reinvestment applies where you dispose of an asset and reinvest the proceeds in the voting shares of an unquoted trading company. A claim is needed and you must acquire the shares within one year before and three years after the disposal.

See also 4.12 etc for wider scope

The new company must carry on a qualifying trade and not be controlled by another company. If it has any subsidiaries, these must be trading and directly owned. Also, the net value of its land must not exceed one-half of its chargeable assets. This is increased to half of its net assets, if more.

Not after 28/11/94. See 4.12

Your replacement expenditure is first allocated to your gain. Thus for full relief, you only need to reinvest your chargeable gain on the old shares and not the entire proceeds.

This relief applies for disposals after 29 November 1993, prior to which (and after 15 March 1993) there was limited relief only. Subject to the rules, disposals only qualified if they themselves consisted of unquoted shares in certain trading companies.

3.21.6

Business retirement relief is available if you are at least 55 and dispose of the whole or part of your business or 'personal company' shares. A 'personal company' is broadly one in which you own at least 5% of the voting shares and are an employee or full-time working officer (including director).

In the case of businesses, only the gain on your 'chargeable business assets' is eligible for relief. Similarly for shares, relief is restricted to a fraction of the gain. This is the ratio of the company's 'chargeable business assets' to its total chargeable assets. Chargeable assets are simply those on which there would be a chargeable gain if sold at a profit.

For maximum relief, ten years' ownership is needed. Otherwise, the full relief is restricted to one-tenth for each complete year of ownership. Full relief consists of the first £250,000 of your gain being free of capital gains tax with only half of the next £750,000 being taxed.

You do not need to retire to obtain the relief. However, if you retire younger than 55 because of ill health, you may be eligible for relief on a disposal of your personal company shares or business. You must give notice within two years of the end of the tax year of the disposal and produce a medical certificate. You need to show that it is unlikely that you will be able to perform your previous work.

3.21.7

Relief for gifts operates by reducing to nil the capital gain on your disposal. At the same time, the recipient's acquisition value of the asset is reduced by your original gain. Both must make a claim for this 'hold-over' treatment within six years of the end of the tax year of the gift. However, if your gift is to a trust, only you need claim.

As the donee, for the relief to be available, you must be UK resident and/or ordinarily resident. If you emigrate within six years of the end of the tax year when you receive a gift, the held-over gain is normally assessed on you.

Only a limited range of gifts qualifies for hold-over relief including:

Shares and securities in family trading companies and non-quoted trading companies.

Business assets used in your trade, profession or vocation, or family company, etc.

Certain agricultural property.

Gifts giving rise to inheritance tax immediately, such as into a discretionary settlement.

Distributions of capital from accumulation and maintenance settlements within the beneficiary's period of entitlement to income.

3.22   Inheritance Tax

3.23   Introduction

Although inheritance tax may arise on certain 'chargeable transfers' during your lifetime, its main impact is on death. At that stage, it may well dwarf any of your earlier income tax or capital gains tax bills. Thus, planning in this area is most important, and is covered later in this book. There follow some basic points about the tax.

3.23.1

A *chargeable transfer* is measured by the decrease in your assets less liabilities which you suffer as a result of the gift, etc. This may be exempted or relieved as later described. If they are not intended to convey any gratuitous benefit, arm's-length transactions are normally ignored. You need to find the fall in the open market value of your 'estate' caused by each transfer, ignoring 'excluded property'.

3.23.2

See 2.21.1 If you are *domiciled* or *deemed domiciled* in the UK, your worldwide property is within the inheritance tax net. Otherwise, only your property situated in this country is covered.

You are *deemed domiciled* in the UK if you have been domiciled here within three years of the chargeable transfer. An alternative test is being UK resident in at least 17 out of the 20 tax years ending with the one when you made the transfer.

3.24 Potentially Exempt Transfers (PETs)

A basic concept of the inheritance tax system is that a wide range of gifts, which are not already exempt, are classed as PETs. This means that the gifts will become exempt unless the donor dies within seven years.

The effect of your making a PET is thus that no inheritance tax will be paid on it unless you die within seven years. However, were that to happen, the PET (less any applicable exemptions) would become taxable, using the rates applicable at death.

Transfers into discretionary settlements are not PETs, nor are certain contrived value transfers regarding close companies. However, gifts, etc. to the following are treated as PETs:

other individuals
accumulation and maintenance settlements
interest in possession trusts
trusts for disabled persons.

3.24.1

Tapering relief is available where you die within seven years of making a PET. Part only of the full tax is payable as follows:

Years between PET and death	% of full tax
0–3	100
3–4	80
4–5	60
5–6	40
6–7	20
7 and over	nil

Where a transfer is within the nil rate band, it attracts no inheritance tax and so tapering relief produces no benefit. As later explained, non-PETs attract tax at half rates and this is increased to the full rates if death occurs within three years. Otherwise, the tapering scale is applied to the rates current at death, but not so as to reduce the original charge.

3.25   Rate Scale

Inheritance tax is chargeable according to the following table. This applies, after 9 March 1992, to chargeable transfers and property passing on death. For earlier periods, different tables have applied, but since 15 March 1988, the rate has been 40%.

Inheritance Tax Rates After 9 March 1992 and before 6 April 1995

1995–6
£154,000

Slice of cumulative chargeable transfers	% on slice
The first £150,000	Nil
The remainder	40

Lifetime gifts which are not PETs are charged at 50% of the full rate. (If death occurs within three years, the full rate is substituted and otherwise the tapering relief scale applies if more tax results.) Such gifts are cumulated with similar transfers within the previous seven years to calculate the amount.

As indicated, a *seven year cumulation period* also operates regarding PETs. Thus, any PETs which you made within seven years of death become chargeable transfers. To find the tax on these PETs, they are cumulated with previous chargeable transfers within seven years of them. The chargeable transfers in the last seven years are then added to the estate at death, in order to compute the tax on this.

3.26 Exempt Transfers

3.26.1

Transfers between husband and wife are normally exempt from inheritance tax. This holds good for lifetime gifts and on death. However, this does *See* not apply if the recipient is not domiciled or deemed domiciled in the *3.23.2* UK, unless the giver is not UK domiciled either. In that case, only £55,000 transferred to the non-domiciled spouse is exempt.

3.26.2

Exempted lifetime gifts can be made as follows by your spouse and yourself:

Transfers each year up to a limit of £3,000. If you do not use up the full £3,000 one tax year, you can carry the unused part to the next year only. However, the exemption for the later year must be used up before the amount brought forward.

For example, if you transfer £1,000 in 1993–4, you carry forward £2,000 of your exemption to 1994–5. Transfers totalling up to £5,000 will then be exempt for 1994–5, but if you only use £3,000, you will have nothing to carry forward.

Small outright gifts not exceeding £250 for each person in any tax year are exempt. However, the £250 exemption cannot be used against gifts larger than that figure. Bigger gifts will need to go against the annual (£3,000) and other exemptions.

• Gifts in consideration of marriage are exempt if made to one of the partners to the marriage or settled for them and their children, etc. The maximum sums exempted depends on the relationship to one or other of the couple. Parents can each give £5,000, grandparents and great-grandparents £2,500, and others £1,000.

• Normal expenditure out of income is exempt, subject to certain conditions. There must be an element of regularity. Also, the transfer must be out of your after-tax income, leaving you with enough income for your usual standard of living.

• Certain gifts for family maintenance purposes are exempt. These include gifts for the maintenance, education, etc. of your child, former spouse and for the maintenance or care of a dependent relative.

3.26.3

Exempt transfers both during life and on death include the following categories, applying for individuals and also trusts:

Transfers in the course of trade, provided they are allowable deductions in computing the profits for income tax purposes.

Gifts of shares to an employee trust provided it will then hold at least half of the ordinary shares of the company.

Gifts to charities and political parties.

Land gifted or sold at under value to housing associations.

Gifts for national purposes made to certain bodies, such as the National Trust and British Museum. Also, gifts for public benefit of property deemed by the Treasury to be of outstanding scenic, historic, artistic or scientific merit.

3.27   Excluded Property

Another category of transfers must be left out of your estate for inheritance tax purposes. This is excluded property such as:

Property outside the UK, provided you are neither domiciled nor deemed domiciled here.

National savings certificates and premium bonds, etc., if you are domiciled in the Channel Islands or the Isle of Man.

There are certain UK Government securities on which interest may be paid gross to non-residents. They are excluded property, provided you are neither UK domiciled nor resident.

Cash options under approved retirement pension schemes, subject to your dependents receiving an annuity, rather than the lump sum.

Certain pensions from former colonies, etc.

Certain reversionary interests, unless purchased.

3.28 Example: Inheritance Tax On a PET

Tim makes a gift to his son of £216,000 on 10 January 1991, having made no chargeable transfers or PETs in the preceding seven years. Tim makes no further PETs or chargeable transfers and dies on 31 March 1995. The inheritance tax payable on the PET will be:

Gift to Tim 10 January 1991		£216,000
Less: Annual exemption 1990–1	3,000	
Annual exemption 1989–90 brought forward	3,000	6,000
		£210,000

Inheritance tax £150,000 at nil%

60,000 at 40%		£24,000

Tapering relief – interval between PET and death 4–5 years

Inheritance tax payable is 60% × £24,000   £14,400

3.29   Inheritance Tax on Death

See 3.23.2

When you die, inheritance tax will be calculated as if you made a chargeable transfer equal to the net value of your estate immediately before your death. This is subject to various adjustments and exemptions. As already mentioned, if you are UK domiciled or deemed domiciled, your worldwide assets are included; otherwise, only those situated here.

The *net value* of your estate is found by making certain deductions from the *gross value*. In turn, that includes all of your assets such as land, shares, debts, etc. Even items only arising after your death, such as life policy proceeds, may need to be included. Also, various types of interests in trusts may need to be included, although the trusts may pay the tax.

The following are among the more common *deductions to be made from the gross estate* in order to arrive at the *net value*:

See 3.26.3 and 3.27

Excluded property and some exempt transfers

Funeral expenses

Certain legal and other professional fees, excluding probate and executor's expenses

UK debts owing at death (see special rules below) and overseas ones, normally only deducted from overseas assets

Liabilities for income tax and capital gains tax up to the date of death, regardless of when the assessments are made.

The inheritance tax payable is calculated from the rate scale, taking account of your cumulative lifetime gifts within seven years of death. As previously mentioned, tax is first calculated on your PETs within seven years of death and tapering relief may apply. Finally, tax is calculated on the estate left at death.

3.30 Example: Inheritance Tax on Death

Tim died on 31 March 1995, having gifted £216,000 to his son on 10 January 1991, as covered in the previous example. His net estate at death was £400,000. Of this, he left £50,000 to charity, £150,000 to his son and the residue, amounting to £200,000, to his wife. Apart from on the £216,000 PET, inheritance tax is payable on the net estate passing at death as follows:

Net estate passing on death		£400,000
Less Legacies to charity £50,000		
Residue to wife	200,000	250,000
Balance taxable		£150,000
Inheritance tax at 40%*		£60,000

* The nil rate band has been fully used against the PET

3.31   Beware of These Special Rules

Among the rules touching on inheritance tax avoidance, the following should particularly be noted.

3.31.1

Associated operations rules enable the Revenue to treat two or more transactions related to the same property as constituting one chargeable transfer. Where the transactions are at different times, the chargeable transfer takes place at the time of the last of them.

3.31.2

Related property is property belonging to your spouse, or which is in a settlement in which he or she has an interest in possession. Also generally included is property which either of you transferred to a charity. Where related property is worth more valued collectively than as the sum of its parts, the higher value applies. This would be likely with unquoted shares, for example.

3.31.3

Debts arising after 17 March 1986 may be prevented from being deducted in whole or in part from your estate at death. An example would be where you had made connected gifts to your creditors. The rules prevent any inheritance tax benefit being obtained, for example, where you give £30,000 to your daughter and borrow back this amount. However, if she lends you £50,000, there would be a deductible debt of £20,000.

3.31.4

Gifts with reservation, subject to the rules, result in the property remaining yours for inheritance tax purposes. This applies where you make a gift after 17 March 1986 and reserve some benefit. A common example is where you gift a house (not to your spouse) but continue living there. If you later release the reservation, that counts as a PET, made at that time.

3.32   Miscellaneous Reliefs

There follow a number of inheritance tax reliefs that are available in certain circumstances. Where relevant, further details are given later in the book.

3.32.1

Land and buildings sold within three years of death for less than their probate value can entitle the person paying the tax to claim relief. (The shortfall must be at least the lower of £1,000 and 5% of the probate value of the land.) Subject to the rules, the sale proceeds are substituted for probate value and the inheritance tax is adjusted.

3.32.2

Quoted securities passing on death, and sold within one year, may attract relief. Those liable to pay the tax can claim to substitute the sale proceeds for the original probate values. The executors are normally liable to pay the inheritance tax and so would need to sell the investments to get the relief. This may be reduced or lost when the proceeds are reinvested in quoted shares within two months after the last sale.

3.32.3

Deeds of variation and disclaimers in respect of property passing on death normally give rise to neither inheritance tax nor capital gains tax. (The effect is to rewrite the will.) They must be executed within two years of the death and an election made to the Revenue within six months of the variation or disclaimer.

Also see 12.16

3.32.4

Double tax relief is available through treaties between the UK and various other countries. These are France, India, Ireland, Italy, Netherlands, Pakistan, South Africa, Sweden, Switzerland and USA. The effect is broadly that property is not taxed both in the UK and the other treaty country. Otherwise, unilateral relief is available, so that overseas tax is set against UK inheritance tax.

3.32.5

Business property relief operates both during life and on death. A reduction is allowed in the value of what is known as 'relevant business property' for inheritance tax purposes, which was owned for at least two years prior to the transfer. The rates of relief on the various types of such property are:

	%
The whole or part of a business	100
Quoted shares to be valued on a control basis	50
Property transferred by you used in a company controlled by you or in your partnership	50
Holding over 25% in an unquoted trading company	100
25% or less in an unquoted trading company	50
Over 25% holding in USM company	100
25% or less without control in USM company	50

In general, investment company shares do not qualify for relief, nor do those in land or share-dealing companies. The relief is given where PETs fall into charge following the donor's death within seven years, provided the property had remained relevant business property. However, the relief is lost if the donee disposes of the property before the donor's death, unless it is replaced by other qualifying assets within three years.

3.32.6

Relief for agricultural property is available where you occupied it for the purposes of agriculture for at least two years before the transfer. Where others do the farming, this period is at least seven years. The rules are relaxed if you inherited or replaced the agricultural property. The relief is 100% if you have vacant possession or can obtain it within 12 months. Otherwise, it is normally 50%, which applies for tenanted situations, etc.

3.32.7

Woodlands relief is available, where owned for at least five years prior to your death or acquired by inheritance or gift. Providing the person inheriting the woodlands so elects within two years, no inheritance tax is paid on it at your death. However, if he or she subsequently sells timber, inheritance tax is charged on this as if it were part of the estate.

3.32.8

Quick succession relief reduces the tax on death where the deceased had received chargeable transfers. Broadly a proportion of the original tax is deducted, being 100, 80, 60, 40 or 20%. These percentages respectively apply where the period between the transfer and death are no more than one, two, three, four or five years.

3.32.9

Waivers of dividends and remuneration to which you are entitled do not give rise to any inheritance tax, subject to the rules. The remuneration would need to have been otherwise liable to income tax under Schedule E and your employer must obtain no tax relief for the waived amount. For dividends, these must be waived within 12 months before being due.

3.33   Collection and Interest

As a rule, chargeable transfers must be reported to the Revenue within 12 months from the end of the month of transfer or death. Before probate is granted, inheritance tax must be paid on at least an estimated estate value.

Unless there is a contrary direction in the will, inheritance tax is payable out of the residuary estate. However, overseas property bears its own tax and that on PETs is the primary responsibility of the recipients.

Inheritance tax on death is due for payment six months from the end of the month of death. For lifetime transfers, the due date is six months after the end of the month of the transfer. Interest at currently 5% (from 6 October 1994) is payable on overdue tax. This is not deductible for income tax purposes.

Inheritance tax at death on certain assets is allowed to be paid by annual instalments over ten years. This applies to controlling shareholdings, certain other unquoted shares, business assets and land and buildings.

Instalments paid on time are generally free of interest apart from on land and buildings not held as business assets, on which interest is paid (5%, etc). Prompt instalments of tax on property qualifying for agricultural relief are interest free.

3.34   Settled Property

The inheritance tax rules regarding settled property are complicated. Some pointers follow and more details are given later in the book.

● In general, where settlements are liable to inheritance tax, it is based on half the full rates. The tax applies on the worldwide assets of a trust, if at the time it was created, the settlor was domiciled in the UK. Otherwise, only assets situated here are included.

● If you settle property, this may be treated as a chargeable transfer. However, settlements on certain trusts are regarded as PETs, so that the property only attracts tax if you die within seven years. Examples are accumulation and maintenance trusts, interest in possession settlements and those for the disabled.

● You have an interest in possession in settled property, where for example you are entitled to receive the income as of right. For inheritance tax purposes, this results in your being treated as owning the property. Thus, tax is payable where the interest in possession ceases as a result of your death. However, if you obtain full ownership of property in which you had an interest in possession, no inheritance tax is payable.

● A selection of trusts are normally exempted from inheritance tax. Examples are charitable trusts, superannuation and other pension schemes, employee trusts, certain 'protective trusts' and trusts for the mentally disabled.

3.34.1

See 7.5 ● *Discretionary settlements* are subjected to special rules, where there is no interest in possession in all or part of the property. These are considered in more detail later. Particularly note that transfers to such settlements are charged at half the normal rates, once cumulative chargeable transfers exceed the nil rate band.

A periodic tax charge arises each tenth anniversary of the creation of the trust. This is based on the property in the trust and is at a maximum of 30% of the lifetime rates. This is proportionately reduced for property not in the settlement for the entire ten-year period. Also, there is an 'exit' charge when capital leaves the trust, calculated on a similar basis.

3.34.2

See 6.14 ● Special treatment applies for *accumulation and maintenance settlements*, as is discussed later in the book. In particular, where no beneficiary is able to obtain an interest in possession until he or she reaches 25 years of age, the trust is not subjected to the periodic charge (see above). No inheritance tax is paid when a beneficiary later obtains such an interest or the capital.

CHAPTER FOUR

November 1994 Budget – Changes and Planning

4.1 Introduction

This chapter is based on the 29 November Budget 1994 changes and related tax-planning points. Account has been taken of the 1995 Finance Bill. However, at the time of writing, Royal Assent has not yet been received and so what follows is only provisional, although material changes are unlikely.

VAT on domestic fuel was to have been increased from 8% to $17\frac{1}{2}$%, but this measure was withdrawn by the Chancellor after being defeated in the Commons. On 8 December, Kenneth Clarke made a statement outlining how he would raise the lost revenue, mainly from duties on road fuel, tobacco and alcohol.

The Budget made many detailed changes to allowances and tax bands, as noted below. But perhaps the most interesting measures relate to capital raising for smaller companies. These include brand new Venture Capital Trusts and important changes to the Enterprise Investment Scheme. Both incorporate highly attractive tax breaks for the investor, so you should consider including them in your tax-saving strategy.

Subjects considered in this chapter include:

73

4.2   Income Tax Rates and Allowances

The income tax rates for 1995–6 remain as before. However, the bands have been widened as follows:

Income Tax Rates 1995–6

Taxable income band £	Tax rate %	Total income £	Total tax £
3,200 (0–3,200)	20	3,200	640
21,100 (3,200–24,300)	25	24,300	5,915
Remainder	40		

4.2.2   Personal Allowances

The main personal allowances have been indexed up for 1995–6, at least in line with inflation. Mortgage relief and married couple's allowance falls from 20% to 15% as previously enacted. However, older couples are compensated by higher increases in their allowances and the age allowance income figure increases from £14,200 to £14,600.

4.2.3 Income Tax Personal Allowances for 1995–6

Type	Relief
	£
Personal allowance	3,525
Additional personal allowance for children	1,720
Blind person's allowance	1,200
Age allowance Age 65–74 at 5 April 1996	4,630
75 and over	4,800
(Reduced by £1 for every £2 over £14,600 down to personal relief level of £3,525)	
Married couple's allowance relieved at 15%:	
Age under 65	1,720
65–74	2,995
75 and over	3,035
Widow's bereavement allowance	1,720
Life assurance relief – percentage of premium (pre-14 March 1984 policies)	12½%
Mortgage interest relief on £30,000 maximum	15%

4.2.4 Planning Implications

The larger income tax allowances and tax rate bands increase the scope for tax saving through income spreading. In particular, bigger trust income distributions can be considered and it becomes more beneficial to split income between spouses. Particular areas involved include:

Children's repayment claims   *6.5*

Accumulation and maintenance trusts   *6.14*

Each individual has £3,525 personal relief for 1995, up £80, £200 more 20% lower rate band and £600 extra 25% basic rate band. This means that an extra £132 tax can be saved if you, as a higher rate payer, arrange for your spouse to have sufficient income to cover his or her personal relief and rate bands. In fact, the extra saving is more if dividend income is involved.

Refer to 8.13 The amount of income that you need to make it worthwhile incorporating from an income tax saving viewpoint has increased. Ignoring allowances except personal relief, you will reach the 40% higher rate threshold at £27,825 (£3,525 + £24,300) for 1995–6, compared with £27,145 (£3,445 + £23,700) for 1994–5.

If you have a family company, the increase in allowances and rate bands enables higher salary and dividend payments to be made without exceeding the 40% income tax rate threshold. This applies both to salary and dividend payments. Again, the combined income level for 1995–6 is £27,825. (This assumes that only personal relief is due.)

Refer to 2.17

4.3   PAYE and Benefits in Kind

Employers whose monthly PAYE and national insurance contributions are less than £450 can pay them over quarterly. For periods ending after 5 April 1995, this limit becomes £600. If you are an employer who qualifies, it is worthwhile considering paying quarterly, in view of the cash-flow advantage and administrative savings.

Where your employer pays liability insurance for you or meets work-related uninsured liabilities, you will no longer be taxed after 5 April 1995. Similarly, if you incur the cost, you will obtain tax relief.

Under the present rules, payments made by your employers for your incidental expenses when away on business trips may be regarded as taxable, since they are not necessary for your employment. Examples are newspapers and telephone calls home. From 6 April 1995, payments up to £5 per day will be tax free (£10 for overseas trips). However, once the limit is exceeded in total for the period away, the whole lot is taxable.

4.4   Company Cars

Refer to 2.17.6– 7

The basic car benefits are now geared to the prices when new and this has not been changed. However, from 1995–6, the costs of converting cars for the disabled are no longer to be included.

The car fuel benefits, which apply if your employer provides you with fuel, are increasing to:

Car Fuel Benefits 1995–96

Cylinder capacity	Petrol £	Diesel £
1,400cc or less	670	605
1,401–2,000cc	850	605
Over 2,000cc	1,260	780

Thus the choice between whether or not to have a company car is still delicately poised. A plus factor may be the employer's improved position regarding VAT input tax, dealt with later in this chapter.

4.5   Changes in Property Taxation

Refer to 2.16

The way that UK property income is taxed is being simplified from 1995–6 for individuals but not companies. Overseas property income taxation for individuals is being aligned with the new UK system, but being kept separate. These changes are being made to facilitate the move to self-assessment, which is effective from 1996–7.

Under the new scheme, income from furnished lettings previously under Schedule D Case 6 will be pooled with other property income under Schedule A. Income and expenses will be based on trading taxation principles, but the net income will be treated as investment rather than trading income.

Existing property losses will be carried forward to offset against your combined property business profits. Similarly, you will be able to carry forward any future losses to set off against subsequent pooled profits. The capital allowance rules will continue where applicable. Also, you will still be able to claim broadly 10% of the rents as wear and tear for furnished lettings.

Interest will be relieved by deducting it like any other expense. If this results as a loss, you will be able to carry it forward. The old requirement that the property must be let or available for letting for at least 26 weeks in a year is going.

From the details available, property investing has certainly been made more attractive from a tax viewpoint. In particular, the removal of the letting requirement makes mortgages more beneficial. Being taxed on one combined property business should make it easier for you to justify the expenses which you claim. Also, it may mean that you can reduce the administration involved, for example on the accounting side.

4.6   Self-Assessment

Refer to 2.5 & 2.18.2 etc The 1994 Budget includes further detailed proposals relating to the new self-assessment system. Although many of these will not take effect until 1996–7, it is wise to plan ahead and ensure that your affairs are sufficiently in order to cope.

4.6.1   Background

The main rules for the revolutionary self-assessment system have already been enacted, although generally they will not take effect until 1996–7. Broadly, you will need to submit your tax return of 1996–7 income by 31 January 1998, together with calculations of your tax liabilities. However, if you submit your return by 30 September 1997, you will not need to send the calculations.

Income tax normally will be payable on account for 1996–7 on 31 January 1997 and 31 July 1997, with any balance on 31 January 1998.

Different rules apply to income taxed at source. Your capital gains tax for 1996–7 will be payable on 31 January 1998.

4.6.2   Budget Changes

For 1996–7 (and subsequently) employers are to give their employees pay and tax details by 31 May 1997. By 6 July 1997, expenses and benefits particulars are to be provided to the employee and the Revenue. The intention is to make it easier for tax returns to be prepared.

In order to ease the introduction of self-assessment from 1996–7, there has been a drive towards simplifying the tax system. Examples in the 1994 Budget include property income (see above) and the UK income of non-residents. For instance, if you are non-resident, UK property income will normally be paid to you less income tax, unless you choose to include it with your payments on account under the self-assessment system.

Also, changes have been made to the rules for taxing income payments to residuary beneficiaries of estates. From 6 April 1995, these are to be taxed in the tax year of receipt, rather than spread over the administration period.

4.6.3   Current Year Basis – Anti-Avoidance

*Refer to
2.18.2*

A far more important example of simplification is the move towards a current year assessment basis for trades (and other Schedule D income). This fully starts from 1997–8 for existing businesses. However, 1996–7 is a transitional year, to be based on half of the profits for the accounts year ending in 1996–7 and half of those for the previous year.

The original rules made it possible to save tax by, for example, switching profits into the two transitional years from the adjoining ones. This might be done by delaying your invoicing, for instance. Profits moved in this way would be reduced by half for tax purposes.

Anti-avoidance rules to counter such schemes were announced in March 1994, for inclusion in the 1995 Finance Bill. Although the rules turn out to be less fierce than those previously announced, you should watch them carefully.

You will not be affected, unless your main object is to save tax by means of the transitional rules. But if you are caught, your 1996–7 assessment is increased by $1\frac{1}{4}$ times the profit which you tried to avoid.

If you are in business as a sole trader or in partnership, this is an area which you should discuss with your accountant. There may still be some scope for saving tax, but the anti-avoidance rules need watching.

Refer to 8.2, 8.12 & 12.2

4.7 Pensions Earnings Cap and Annuities

The pensions schemes earnings cap has been increased from £76,800 to £78,600 from 6 April 1995. This is the maximum level of earnings for which pension provision with tax relief can be made. It applies where you contribute to a personal pension scheme, joined an occupational scheme after 31 May 1989 or one set up since 19 March 1989.

If you have high earnings, the increased cap will allow you to increase your pension contributions from 1995–6. Thus, if you are at least 61 on 6 April 1995, the £1,800 increase in the cap will put up your personal pensions contributions limit by 40% × £1,800 = £720 for 1995–6.

The position regarding drawing annuities from personal pension schemes is to improve subject to approval being obtained under the 1995 Finance Act. The new arrangements will allow you to defer purchasing your pension annuity until you are not older than 75. This applies whether or not you take your tax-free lump sum. At the same time, you will be allowed to make income withdrawals from the fund commensurate with the annuity you would have obtained.

The new rules will help you if annuity rates are low when you reach your normal pension age. Also, if the fund value is low due to market factors, deferral might be advantageous. So you should make sure that the schemes to which you belong and which you join will be suitably empowered.

Refer to 9.13.6

4.8 Enterprise Investment Scheme (EIS)

The EIS has been running since January 1994, but changes made by the 1994 Budget make it far more attractive. The changes take effect from 29 November 1994 and include:

Introducing capital gains tax reinvestment relief for capital gains reinvested in EIS shares.

Abolishing the rule which broadly denies relief where a company's land and buildings are more than half of its assets.

Abolishing the parallel trades rule denying relief where similar trades are carried on by companies under common control.

The existing 20% relief against your income continues for your EIS share purchases, as does capital gains tax exemption. Of course, you need to hold the shares for at least five years. Thus the scope for companies to qualify has become wider and the relief for investors much better.

Capital gains tax reinvestment relief applies to assets which you realise after 28 November 1994. Also the general rule applies, that your EIS shares must be purchased within three years after and one year before the disposals.

The effect of obtaining reinvestment relief is striking. Suppose that for 1994–5 you have a capital gain of £20,000, on which you would otherwise pay 40% tax. If you buy EIS shares for £20,000 after 28 November 1994 (and within three years after your disposal), your capital gain is deferred until you sell your EIS shares.

The result is that £8,000 of capital gains tax is sheltered. At the same time, 20% (£4,000) relief is set against your income tax liability. So your immediate relief (subject to holding for five years) is 60% although part is merely the result of deferring your gain.

Thus, investing in EIS shares is highly tax effective and you can do this up to a maximum of £100,000 each tax year. But you should be aware of their speculative nature. Also consider venture capital trust shares, which offer similar tax advantages and are discussed next.

4.9   Venture Capital Trusts (VCTs)

The VCT scheme operates from 6 April 1995. VCTs must be quoted on the Stock Exchange and this represents one of their main advantages as an investment and tax-planning tool. In general, EIS shares do not have so easy and flexible an 'exit route'.

4.9.1 The Rules for the VCT Company

VCTs will need to invest as to at least 70% in unquoted trading companies, with not more than 15% in any one company or group. A VCT can hold shares, or loans with a life of at least five years. However, at least 50% of the investments must be in ordinary shares. Initially three years will be allowed to meet the 70% and 50% requirements.

No investment in a company counts towards the 70% unquoted trading company requirement if its gross assets exceed £10m. Furthermore, a VCT can invest no more than £1m into each such company in any year. Thus, the companies are fairly small and there is undoubtedly a degree of risk, hence good management is most desirable.

4.9.2 VCTs and the Investor

To compensate for the risk involved, the tax breaks for the investor in VCTs are huge. The main conditions are that you subscribe for new ordinary shares and hold them for at least five years. You are allowed to invest up to £100,000 each tax year from 6 April 1995. The tax benefits comprise:

  20% relief to set against your income tax bill
  Freedom from income tax on your VCT dividends
  Exemption for capital gains tax on selling your VCTs
  Reinvestment relief for other gains.

You can obtain reinvestment relief, when you subscribe for VCT shares, within one year before and one year after your disposal, similar to that for EIS shares (see above). By investing gains on other assets in VCT shares, you shelter the amount covered until you sell. Hence you obtain a deferment of the capital gains tax as well as your 20% income tax relief on the entire amount you subscribe. This can amount to 60% in all (20% + 40%) where you are a top rate tax payer and shelter capital gains at least equal to your subscription.

4.9.3 Your VCT and EIS Tax-Planning Strategy

Regarding 1994–5, only EIS shares are available, which if purchased before 6 April 1995 provide 20% income tax relief on your investment. This is worth having, if you are happy about the particular EIS companies you invest in and can afford to hold the shares for at least five years.

Another important point to consider is how easy it is to realise your investment after the five-year period ends. Different arrangements apply to particular EIS companies. As mentioned, this constraint does not apply for VCTs, since they are to be saleable on the Stock Exchange. However, the prices will naturally fluctuate and you may wish to delay selling after the five years.

Thus, for flexibility and liquidity, from 1995–6, when both will be available, it seems wisest to invest first in VCT shares. However, there may be special reasons, such as personal knowledge of an EIS company, which might decide you to invest in it.

The total possible investment which you can make for 1994–5 is £100,000 in EIS shares and from 1995–6 £200,000 each tax year (£100,000 EIS and £100,000 VCT). This will reduce your income tax bill by £40,000 if your income is high enough. However, if you are making large VCT and EIS investments, it is wise to diversify, so that you spread the risk between a number of companies.

But the most dramatic tax-planning use for both EIS and VCT investment is in the field of capital gains tax. This is equally true with smaller or larger capital gains. The following broad comments are subject to the detailed rules.

If you make capital gains on your Stock Exchange investments these can be sheltered by reinvesting in VCT or EIS shares. On the other hand, if you have a really large gain, say on selling your family company, here too such reinvestment can be used to shelter all or part of the gain.

You must look at the position after deducting your annual exemption. For example, suppose you have net gains less losses for 1995–6 of £16,000. Deducting your annual exemption of £6,000 leaves £10,000, which you could defer by subscribing this amount for VCT (or EIS) shares. In cash terms, it will be a question of subscribing only part of your share proceeds.

If you are a 40% taxpayer, your 1995–6 tax liabilities will be reduced by 40% capital gains tax (£4,000) and 20% income tax (£2,000). After five years, you will be able to sell your VCT shares on the Stock Exchange and if they do well, you will have a tax-free capital gain. Of course, your original deferred capital gain will be taxable, subject to the rules and rates then existing.

There are various ways in which you should be able to relieve the deferred gains when you realise your VCT shares. You might 'bed and breakfast' shares to make capital losses to offset. Alternatively, you could split your VCT share sales between two tax years and thus use your annual exemptions for both years.

When it comes to larger capital gains, you may already have other forms of relief. Examples are business retirement relief and relief for reinvestment in non-quoted trading companies. Also, where you are selling your company, another possibility is a paper for paper deal to defer the capital gains. To the extent that these are not appropriate, VCT and EIS shares offer much scope.

For example, suppose you plan to sell your company for £5m in July 1995 and anticipate a capital gain of £800,000 in total. If you own all of the shares, you could transfer half to your spouse now, so that you each expect a capital gain of £400,000 on sale.

If you are in time, you could invest £100,000 each in EIS shares after 28 November 1994 and before 6 April 1995. In 1995–6, both of you will be able to make combined EIS and VCT investments of £200,000. A further £100,000 each early in 1996–7, will complete the cover. Under the rules, all of these investments fall within the time limits.

In all, your spouse and yourself will have invested £800,000 between you in EIS and VCT shares, leaving £4,200,00 free out of the £5m proceeds. In addition, there is 20% income tax relief provided your respective incomes are sufficient.

The above comments are intended to alert you to some of the interesting tax-saving possibilities in this new field. But complex matters are involved and you should seek good advice, both on the technical and investment sides.

4.10 PEPs and TESSAs

EIS and VCT shares actually reduce your tax on other sources of income, but are speculative as explained above. With TESSAs and PEPs, the speculative element is less, but the tax benefits are confined to the investments themselves.

PEPs were introduced on 1 January 1987 and TESSAs four years later. Improvements are now to be made in each case. For PEPs, the range of investments is being widened early in 1995–6.

As the name implies, investment by *personal equity plans* (PEPs) has been broadly confined to UK and EC ordinary shares and certain unit and investment trusts. The extensions cover specified corporate bonds and convertibles of UK non-financial companies; also preference shares in UK and EC companies. (All investments must be in quoted companies.)

Unit and investment trusts holding at least half of their assets in ordinary and preference shares will qualify, so that the remainder could be in corporate bonds. In that case, the capital gains tax-saving advantage of the PEP will be reduced, since corporate bonds are generally exempt in any case. However, the tax-free income element of such a PEP is likely to prove more durable and secure.

An even safer form of tax-efficient investment is through a *tax exempt special saving account* (TESSA), with a bank or building society. The five-year holding period means the first TESSAs will be maturing in January 1996.

Under current rules, when your TESSA matures, you would be able to put up to £3,000 into a new one, with the usual subsequent £1,800 annual maximum and £9,000 total limit.

The new rules allow you to invest the capital (not interest) of your existing TESSA into a new one. You will have up to six months in which to do this, in which case you will continue to obtain tax-free income.

If you put less than £9,000 into your new TESSA, you will be able to make up the balance yearly, subject to the £1,800 annual limit. Where you have not previously held a TESSA or have less than £3,000 in one which is maturing, your first-year limit is £3,000.

As discussed elsewhere, the chance to generate tax-free income from a secure source is one of which you should take advantage, if you have spare funds. The new rules mean that if you already have a TESSA, you will be able to arrange for your tax-free income to continue with little or no interruption. Otherwise, consider opening one.

Refer to 3.6

4.11   Capital Gains Tax Reliefs

Refer to 4.8 & 4.9

The main improvements to the capital gains tax reliefs brought about by the 1994 Budget are in the field of reinvestment relief. This is covered above concerning EIS and VCT investment. Other changes are dealt with below.

Some capital gains tax relief has resulted from the improved income tax scale. Thus, the first £3,200 of your income (or gains) is taxed at 20% for 1995–6 instead of £3,000, £21,000 being at 25% (up £400). This means that if your income has not absorbed all of your lower and basic rate tax bands, more of your capital gains will be taxed at lower rates than 40%.

In a similar way, the increase in the annual capital gains tax exempt amount by £200 to £6,000 for 1995–6 slightly reduces the burden of the tax. The exempt amounts for trusts, etc. also increase as follows:

Capital Gains Tax – Exempt Amounts 1995–6

	£
Individuals	6,000
Personal representatives (tax year of death and next two), trusts for the mentally handicapped and for those receiving attendance allowance	6,000
Other trusts, such as accumulation and maintenance and discretionary ones (maximum)	3,000
Minimum exemption for each A & M or discretionary trust set up by the same settlor after 6 June 1978	300

The increases are in line with indexation, and you should keep them in mind regarding various tax-planning exercises. An example is where you 'bed and breakfast' (sell and repurchase) shares in 1995–6 so as to create gains within the £6,000 limit.

Both the new annual exemption and tax band increases should be taken into account when planning for gains to be realised within your family. There is a little more scope for you to save tax by transferring assets to your spouse, so that the 1995–6 capital gains are his or hers.

4.12   Capital Gains Tax Reinvestment Relief

Refer to 3.21.5

This relief was first introduced where you disposed of certain shares in unquoted trading companies and reinvested the proceeds in similar companies, subject to the rules. This was from 16 March 1993, and from 30 November 1993 this rolling over facility was extended to other asset disposals.

As seen earlier in this chapter, forms of reinvestment relief have now been introduced using EIS and VCT shares. In addition, from 29 November 1994, two important relaxations take effect regarding the existing scheme.

The rule has been abolished under which the proportion of land which a qualifying company could hold was limited to half the value of its assets. Other restrictions being removed cover the trades in which reinvestment companies may emerge. In particular, property development and farming now are satisfactory trades.

Unless there are special reasons for your buying ordinary shares in an unquoted company, for general investment and tax saving, VCT shares would appear to offer more. However, you may have personal connections with the company. At all events, the new relaxations should greatly increase the number of companies affording reinvestment relief.

Refer to 3.25 ## 4.13 Inheritance Tax

The 1994 Budget contains the first increase in the inheritance tax nil-rate band since 9 March 1992. The amount is raised by £4,000 for chargeable transfers after 5 April 1995, when the rate scale is as follows:

Inheritance Tax Rates After 5 April 1995

Slice of cumulative chargeable transfers	*% on slice*
The first £154,000	Nil
The remainder	40

Using the nil-rate band forms an important part of planning regarding inheritance tax. Thus, you should consider the increase with regard to various matters covered in this book, such as wills, lifetime gifts and setting up discretionary settlements.

For example, suppose you have drawn up your will so as to leave the nil-rate band to your children and the remainder to your spouse. A further £4,000 is now available and you could alter your will accordingly, leaving £154,000 to your children.

Most lifetime gifts are potentially exempt, so that inheritance tax is only payable if you die within seven years. However, it is comforting to keep your gifts within your nil-rate band and exemptions. If you have been doing this to the full, you will have a further £3,000 annual exemption and £4,000 extra nil-rate band available to gift in 1995–6. This makes £7,000, ignoring any other reliefs.

When you settle money on discretionary trusts, inheritance tax is chargeable at half the full 40% rate. It is thus desirable to keep within the nil-rate band and the increase to £154,000 is of modest help.

Inheritance tax planning is generally for the longer term and so the political factor needs constantly to be kept in mind. Were there to be a change in Government, a more severe system might be introduced. The possibility of this happening is brought home by the parliamentary defeat and withdrawal of the intended VAT increase on domestic fuel. This now seems to be a good time for you to check out your inheritance tax strategy.

4.14   VAT

Refer to 8.10 & App. 15

The Budget contains various proposals relating to VAT, most of which are outside the scope of this book. As mentioned above, the previously enacted increase in the rate on domestic fuel to 17.5% has been cancelled. The rates and registration thresholds are now as follows:

Value Added Tax Rates, Etc.

Standard VAT rate	17.5%
VAT rate on domestic fuel and power	8.0%
Registration threshold after 29 November 1994 (annual turnover)	£46,000
Deregistration threshold after 29 November 1994	£44,000

The car fuel benefits shown earlier in this chapter also apply for VAT purposes, with corresponding monthly and quarterly figures. Also concerning cars, changes have been announced which are expected mainly to affect the leasing market, although other businesses may benefit.

Refer to 4.4

From 1 August 1995, where a business purchases cars *wholly* for business purposes (including leasing them out) the input tax will be recoverable. However, those businesses will have to charge VAT when they sell the cars.

A new rule will also apply if your business leases a car from a leasing concern which has recovered input tax on the purchase as above. Where there is any private motoring use of the car, only 50% of the VAT on the leasing cost will be recoverable.

Refer to
App. 16

4.15   National Insurance Contributions

The national insurance contribution levels have been changed from 6 April 1995. These need to be taken into account in planning areas such as whether to incorporate, and salary levels.

Refer to
8.13

A particular point to note is that employers' contributions for all employees earning less than £205 weekly are cut by 0.6%. This is to encourage the employment of the lower paid.

A further proposed measure is to start in April 1996. Employers taking on people who have been out of work for at least two years will get up to one year's full national insurance contributions rebate for each.

The full table follows and you should note that the 'lower earnings limit' (LEL) was announced as £59 in the Budget. However, it was later reduced to £58 as part of the package of measures to compensate for holding the rate of VAT on domestic fuel at 8%.

National Insurance Contribution Rates for 1995–6

	Employee £	Employer £
'Class 1' – employees aged 16 and over:		
Lower earning limit (LEL) per week	58.00	
Upper earning limit (UEL) per week	440.00	
(a) earnings less than LEL	Nil	Nil
(b) earnings LEL or more and contracted out	see below	
(c) earnings at least LEL and contracted in	see below	
'Class 2' – self-employed pw (LEL £3,310)	5.85	
'Class 3' – voluntary contributions pw	5.75	
'Class 4' – self-employed earnings related	7.3% of profits between £6,640 and £22,880	

Class 1 Contributions

Employee	*Not contracted-out*	*Contracted-out*
	%	%
Weekly earnings below £58	Nil	Nil
Weekly earnings from £58:		
£0–£57.99	2	2
£58–440	10	8.2
Over £440	No further liability	

Employer	*Not contracted-out*	*Contracted-out*	
	%	*% on*	*% on*
Weekly earnings		*First £58*	*Remainder*
Under £58	Nil	Nil	Nil
£58–104.99	3	3	Nil
£105–149.99	5	5	2
£150–204.99	7	7	4
£205–440	10.2	10.2	7.2
Over £440	10.2	10.2	7.2 on £382
			10.2 on excess

The lower earnings limit for Class 1 contributions is a key figure for tax-planning purposes. The increase from £57 per week for 1994–5 to £58 for 1995–6 is slight but it does mean that the annual equivalent has moved above £3,000.

Thus, you might pay your spouse or children annual salaries of say £3,000 each for work they do in your business without any national insurance contributions arising. Similarly, if you have a number of companies you could restrict your salaries from some of them in this way.

4.16   The Overall Budget Picture

The overall picture presented by the Budget is that it makes few changes to the basic rules relating to tax planning as described in this book. However, many of the numbers have been indexed up as described above and so these should be taken account of in your planning.

As always, new anti-avoidance measures are being introduced. These include the artificial avoidance of VAT on property transactions and share issues, stopping purchasing companies in order to use their surplus management expenses and operations with discounted securities. Always seek expert advice if you are contemplating sophisticated tax-avoidance operations.

So far as officially approved tax-planning tools are concerned, the Budget contains details of two highly tax-efficient investments. These are venture capital trusts and revamped enterprised investment shares. They are certainly both Budget highlights and worthy of your serious attention.

Refer to 4.8 & 4.9

PART TWO

The Seven Ages of Tax Planning

All the world's a stage,
And all the men and women merely players;
They have their exits and their entrances;
And one man in his time plays many parts,
His acts being *seven ages*.

As You Like It, William Shakespeare

CHAPTER FIVE

Introduction

The previous chapters have provided background information to tax planning; in particular, the main taxes are covered in outline. The next seven chapters deal with tax planning at different stages in your life, the 'seven ages'. These are:

Childhood
Student days
Early working life
Newly married
Parenthood
Middle age
Retirement.

Where sufficient technical background has not been previously given, the aim is to include this with the planning suggestions.

This part of the book is designed for you to go straight to your particular 'age' for suggested tax planning relevant to you. However, if you have one or more children or grandchildren, the 'childhood' chapter will be very relevant. Also, if you have retired parents, you may wish to turn to the 'retirement' chapter.

You should also plan to read all of the seven chapters, particularly covering the 'ages' starting with your own. This should help your long-term planning. It is important to plan for the longer as well as shorter term.

Note that as your progress through the various 'ages', your involvement will be completely passive to begin with. In other words, as a child, your parents and grandparents, etc. would make any tax-planning arrangements for you.

As time passes on, you are likely to take an increasingly active role, as is seen in the following chapters. You may well be making arrangements to benefit not only your spouse, but also future generations. However, it may be that later in life, your part becomes more passive again. The various chapters thus deal with what is to be done both by and for particular people.

The selected ages are fairly typical, being largely chronological. They certainly do not correspond exactly with Shakespeare. In fact, he adds an extra dimension, by telling us something about our hero at each 'age' in his life. So let's see how Shakespeare described the 'seven ages'.

> As first the infant,
> Mewling and puking in the nurse's arms.
> And then the whining school-boy, with his satchel
> And shining morning face,
> creeping like snail unwillingly to school.
> And then the lover, sighing like a furnace,
> With a woeful ballad made to his mistress' eyebrow.
> Then the soldier, full of strange oaths
> And bearded like the pard,
> Jealous in honour, sudden and quick in quarrel,
> Seeking the bubble reputation, even in the cannon's mouth.
> And then the justice in fair round belly with good capon lined,
> With eyes severe and beard of formal cut,
> Full of wise saws and modern instances;
> And so he plays his part.
> The sixth age shifts into the lean and slipper'd pantaloon,
> With spectacles on nose and pouch on side;
> His youthful hose, well sav'd,
> A world too wide for his shrunk shank;
> And his big manly voice turning again toward childish treble,
> Pipes and whistles in his sound.
> Last scene of all, that ends this strange eventful history,
> Is second childishness and mere oblivion,
> Sans teeth, sans eyes, sans every thing.

Remember that 'one man in his time plays many parts'. Thus Shakespeare is suggesting that the whining schoolboy becomes the lover and then the wild soldier, before being a justice. Thus, your 20-year-old son may be completely irresponsible and not to be trusted with money. But do not abandon all thoughts of passing property to him. He may turn out to be a very solid citizen in the future.

Where your children are still in their formative years, trusts of various kinds can be most useful. For instance, they enable the children to reach maturity before funds are released to them. They also produce valuable tax savings, as is later described.

Another timely message from the Shakespeare quotation is that not only your character changes but also your job might change. In recent years, partly due to economic factors, job mobility has increased, with people remaining in particular jobs for shorter periods than before. Thus, you should allow sufficient flexibility in your tax planning and financial arrangements to deal with job changes and perhaps setting up on your own.

Finally, you should note the 'last scene of all', second childishness. If at all possible, you should provide for this contingency by having adequate health insurance and funds put aside. As a last resort and if your children can be depended upon, you may be able to look to them to cover any shortfall.

CHAPTER SIX

Childhood

6.1

I often think it comical
How Nature always does contrive
That every boy and every gal
That's born into the world alive
Is either a little Liberal
Or else a little Conservative!

This is from *Iolanthe* by Gilbert and Sullivan and, if of doubtful authenticity then, is even less true now. However, a far more striking feature of the newly born is that they each have a full set of tax allowances. They may not have full sets of teeth, or indeed any at all, but they each have the same basic tax allowances as an adult.

In fact, a wide variety of tax planning is appropriate concerning children and this chapter covers this field, including:

100

From the day a baby is born, he or she has the benefit of an array of tax allowances. Examples are given below.

___

6.2 Some Tax Reliefs From Birth

	1994–5	1995–6	
Income Tax	£	£	
personal allowance	3,445	3,525	See 2.5–9
lower rate band at 20%	3,000	3,200	
basic rate band at 25%	20,700	21,100	
Capital gains tax			
annual exemption	5,800	6,000	See 3.2
Inheritance tax			
annual exemption	3,000	3,000	See 3.25–6
nil rate band	150,000	154,00	

___

6.3   Using The Income Tax Allowances

One of the techniques of tax planning for children is to put them in a position to use their allowances from an early age. This involves making gifts and settlements so that they obtain the income.

One snag is that if you gift assets to your children, the income is treated as yours for tax purposes. The same applies if you settle assets, and your children are paid income from the trust. However, once any child comes of age (18 years), he or she and not you is taxed on the income. This also applies if the child is married. Where the income involved for a minor child is no more than £100 in the tax year, it is not assessed on you.

Thus, where possible, grandparents and others should make gifts and settlements to your children so you are not assessed on the income. The children will then be able to benefit from their tax allowances, claiming back part or all of the tax suffered at source.

Another way that your children can use up their tax allowances and lower rate band (20%) is against their wages. If they have none, then there may be scope for them to have occasional *employment through your business*. However, they must really work and the arrangements should not be artificial.

6.4   Deeds of Covenant

Some children may still be receiving annual income under deeds of covenant. If these were effected prior to 15 March 1988, the payments are made under the deduction of basic rate income tax. This tax can be reclaimed on behalf of each child to the extent that there are unused allowances. Of course, this does not apply where you covenanted to pay your child and he or she is still a minor.

Deeds of covenant were deprived of their tax advantages if executed after 14 March 1988 (except for charities). However, existing ones still attract relief. The common type of pre-15 March 1988 covenant ran for seven annual payments only and normally would have expired by now. But some run on until, say, the child reaches 18 or 21, or completes full-time education. If your children enjoy payments under deeds of covenant like that, it is important to keep them going as long as possible.

6.5 Example: Repayment Claim for Child

Polly is ten years old. For the tax year 1994–5, she has the following taxed income:

	Gross £
Annual payment under deed of covenant from grandfather	3,000
Bank deposit interest (capital gifted by grandmother)	800
Dividends on shares gifted by father	250
Dividends on shares gifted by great aunt	1,000

The dividends from her father will be taxed on him and not Polly. She will have a repayment claim for 1994–5 as shown.

	Gross (£)	Income tax deducted or tax credits (£)
Deed of covenant payments	3,000	750
Bank deposit interest	800	200
Dividends (tax credit 20%)	1,000	200
Total income	4,800	1,150
Less personal allowance	3,445	
Taxable amount	1,355	
Income tax due £1,355 at 20%		271
Less income tax suffered by deduction at source and tax credits		1,150
Net income tax reclaimable		879

6.6   Asset Ownership

In general, your children can own assets in their own names. However, a small number of limited companies do not allow their shares to be transferred to minors and a trustee may be needed. The main area where there are problems is regarding land and buildings. Until a child reaches majority (age 18) a trust arrangement normally will be required.

Another vital factor to consider is whether the children are sufficiently responsible to own wealth outright. In many cases, it will be more sensible for trusts to be involved. These can be used to own investments and other assets until the children are more responsible. This is discussed later.

6.7   Capital Gains Tax

1995–6
£6,000
A child has the full annual exemption for capital gains tax. This is currently £5,800. Also, the chattels exemption of £6,000 applies, although this is not likely to be so useful.

Note that you are not automatically taxed on the capital gains realised by your child on assets you had given him or her. The income tax rule mentioned above is not mirrored in the capital gains tax rules. However, there is a risk that the Revenue might try to follow that path in very artificial circumstances.

An example would be where you gift shares in your family company to your son, making an election to hold over the gain, and he sells them immediately. The Revenue might invoke various anti-avoidance case *See 1.2* decisions, such as in 'Ramsay'. So if you intend making such gifts, do so well in advance of any anticipated future sale.

Remember that if you gift an asset to your child, this may result in your having a capital gain. However, you may be able to make a joint hold-over election regarding certain assets, such as family company shares.

Apart from the £5,800 annual exemption, also remember the lower and basic rate bands. The first £3,000 will be taxed at only 20% and £20,700 at 25% before the 40% level is reached. These rates apply first to the taxable income and then the capital gains. However, a child's income will *See 6.2*
for
1995–6
details often be no more than the £3,445 personal allowance. In that case, the full 20% lower rate and 25% basic rate bands will be available against the child's capital gains.

It follows that if you envisage substantial capital gains in the future, you should consider passing assets over to your children well in advance. This particularly applies to shares and, ideally, they can be purchased in the children's names in the first place.

6.8 Example: Child's Capital Gain

George starts a new company and subscribes for 10% of the ordinary share in the name of his 11-year-old son Percy. Five years later, in 1994–5, he sells the entire company and is well into the 40% band on his income and gains. The capital gain on Percy's shares is £30,000 and his income for 1994–5 only £3,000.

Since Percy's income for 1994–5 is less than his personal allowance (£3,445), his entire lower rate and basic rate bands will be available against his capital gain. Tax will be payable as follows:

Chargeable gain on sale of shares		£30,000
Less: Annual exemption		5,800
		£24,200
Capital gains tax payable:	£3,000 at 20%	600
	20,700 at 25%	5,175
	500 at 40%	200
TOTAL CAPITAL GAINS TAX		£5,975

Note that had George kept Percy's 10% holding, his extra capital gains tax would have been £30,000 × 40% = £12,000. Thus, by Percy owning these shares, there has been a tax saving of £12,000 – 5,975 = **£6,025**

6.9   Inheritance Tax

As soon as a child is born, he or she becomes a player in the inheritance tax game, if at first a purely passive one. As mentioned, the full rate scale and reliefs are available for making transfers. However, young children are far more likely to feature as beneficiaries, rather than givers.

Without your doing anything, a child automatically may be born into existing tax-planning arrangements. For example, there may be a trust which includes your issue as beneficiaries. In any event, consider including the child in your will, if this is appropriate.

1995–6
£61,600
£154,000

With the present rules, up to £60,000 inheritance tax can be saved by leaving money direct to your children rather than to your spouse. This comes about through using all or part of the £150,000 nil rate band, which otherwise might be wasted.

6.10 Example: Using The Nil Rate Band

Jack and Jill originally made out their wills leaving all of their estates to the survivor. They now each include their son James with a legacy of £150,000 on the first death. Assuming that each has £250,000, Jack dies first, ignoring fluctuations up to Jill's death and using the 1994–5 rates, the inheritance tax will be:

Under the original wills	*Jack*	*Jill*
	£	£
Net estates at Jack's death	250,000	250,000
Inheritance tax (all estate left to surviving spouse)	NIL	
Estate passing to Jill	(250,000)	250,000
Net estate at Jill's death		500,000
Inheritance tax payable:	150,000	NIL
	350,000 at 40%	140,000

Under the new wills	*Jack*	*Jill*
Net estates at Jack's death	250,000	250,000
Inheritance tax (£150,000 to James is covered by the nil rate band and the remainder left to the surviving spouse)	NIL	
Legacy to James	(150,000)	
Estate passing to Jill	(100,000)	100,000
Net estate at Jill's death		350,000

Inheritance tax payable:	150,000	NIL
	200,000 at 40%	80,000

Thus, by changing the wills, inheritance tax of
£140,000 – 80,000 = £60,000 has been saved

6.11   Lifetime Gifts For Children

Once your first child is born, there is scope for passing wealth to him or
her. Of course, this is subject to the practicalities of ownership by children
that are discussed above.

There are three basic stages. Gifts can be made out of the exemptions
and, in particular, the annual £3,000 from you, your spouse and the
grandparents. Above that, there is the inheritance tax nil rate band of at
present £150,000. Above that, if you are really wealthy, you could consider
gifts to your children far above the nil rate band. Larger gifts are best made
in trust.

1995–6
£154,000

Apart from transfers to discretionary settlements, most other gifts in excess
of the exemptions would normally be PETs. Thus, they would only be
taxable if the donor dies within seven years. (The inheritance tax arising
in this eventuality can be covered by life assurance comparatively cheaply.)

Under the present rules, the PETs will be safe from possible inheritance
tax once seven years have passed. You can then consider further large gifts
to your children out of the renewed nil rate band. Hence the value of
starting the process early.

6.12 Example: Lifetime Gifts For Children

Bill is very wealthy and Jane, his first child, is born on 1 June 1994. He decides to take
full advantage of the inheritance tax nil rate band and annual exemption. He creates
an accumulation and maintenance settlement for Jane and any future children.

Assume that he has not previously touched his nil rate band and annual exemptions
and that these remain in the future at their 1994–5 levels. He will be able to put
the following amounts into the settlement covered by these items:

Out of nil rate band on say	1 July 1994	£150,000
	1 July 2001	150,000
	1 July 2008	150,000
	1 July 2015	150,000
From annual exemptions say 26 × £3,000*		78,000
Total added to settlement		£678,000

Notes

* Unused annual exemption has been carried forward from 1993–4 and included up to 2019–20. On 1 June 2020, Jane reaches age 25 and so no further such settlements can be made for her. However, direct gifts to her can be considered.

From the above, £78,000 is exempt and £600,000 PETs. If Bill were to die after 1 July 2022, the entire £678,000 will escape charge. However, had he not made the above transfers, an extra £678,000 would come into charge, on which the inheritance tax would be £678,000 × 40% = £271,200.

Bill's wife Peggy is able to make transfers of identical amounts and so the overall potential saving is £542,400.

6.13   What Are Trusts?

Indicating their great value in tax planning, trusts have been mentioned on various earlier pages of this book. The time is thus overdue for a word of explanation. A trust is created when a person (the settlor) transfers assets to trustees for the benefit of third parties (beneficiaries). Trusts are also broadly known as settlements.

You may create a trust under the terms of your will, to take effect when you die. You would do this by setting aside all or part of your estate to be administered by trustees for the benefit of your heirs and other beneficiaries.

The key to any trust is the trust deed. This states who the settlor is and gives details of the trustees and beneficiaries. It also describes the assets being settled and gives the rules of the trust. Drawing up trust deeds is definitely a job for your solicitor. The most common types of settlement used for tax planning purposes are:

Accumulation and maintenance (considered below) *See 6.14*

Discretionary (where the application of the income and/or capital is left *See 7.5* to the discretion of the trustees)

Interest in possession (for example where you receive the income as of right)

Bare trusts (considered later this chapter in their application to minors). *See 6.16*

Now a note of warning about the tax consequences of certain trusts. You will be assessed to tax on the income of a trust of which you are the settlor if you or your spouse has the right to receive income or capital. However, this does not apply if your spouse is only able to benefit after you die. Another case is where your unmarried minor children (under 18) receive income, but you will not be assessed on accumulated income.

6.14 Accumulation and Maintenance Trusts

Accumulation and maintenance settlements enable the income to be paid out for the maintenance and education of minor beneficiaries and otherwise. To the extent that the income is not paid out, it is accumulated and is available for future distribution.

Provided the following conditions are satisfied, valuable inheritance tax relief is obtained. In fact, it is strongly recommended that if you use an accumulation and maintenance settlement, it will comply with these conditions.

● All beneficiaries will obtain interests in possession by the time they reach their twenty-fifth birthdays. Thus by that time, they need to be entitled to all or part of the income.

● No one yet has an interest in possession in the trust fund.

● Either not more than 25 years have passed since the original settlement date or all of the beneficiaries are grandchildren of a common grandparent. This extends to their widows, widowers, children, stepchildren, etc.

Subject to these conditions, no inheritance tax is payable during the life of the trust, nor when beneficiaries become entitled to income or capital. Furthermore, when you create the trust, any cash and other assets that you settle will be PETs. Thus no inheritance tax can be payable on them unless you die within seven years.

Regarding the age when beneficiaries should be entitled to their shares of the capital, this can be stipulated in the trust deed as being, say, 25 or 35. Alternatively, it can be left to the discretion of the trustees, normally with a stated minimum age.

See 7.5   So far as *other taxes* are concerned, special rules apply for both income tax and capital gains tax. These are the same as for discretionary settlements.

In general, an *additional income tax rate of 10%* applies, on top of the 25% basic rate. However, this is not the case where the income belongs to a beneficiary as of right. Another exception is where you are the settlor and the income is treated as your own for tax purposes.

The overall income tax rate is 35% (25 + 10), but often the investment income received will have been taxed at source. Thus, dividends received carry a tax credit of 20% and bank or building society income normally 25%.

Trust management expenses are relieved only against the additional rate, but there is a special rule. They are first allocated to dividend income, where they produce relief of 15% (35 – 20). Any excess goes against other income, producing 10% relief (35 – 25).

6.14.1 Example: Accumulation And Maintenance Trust Income Tax

The income of an accumulation and maintenance trust for 1994–5 consists of:
dividends £8,000 (tax credits £2,000)
bank interest £7,500 (net of income tax £2,500)
management expenses £6,000.

Income tax is payable as follows:

	Gross income	*Tax credits*
Bank interest	10,000	2,500
Dividends	10,000	2,000
	£20,000	£4,500
Income tax at 35% on £20,000		7,000
Less: Management expenses £6,000 at 15%	900	
Tax credits	4,500	5,400
Net further income tax payable		£1,600

Income distributions to beneficiaries are treated as being net of 35% income tax. This includes where payments are made for the maintenance and education of children. Depending on the other income of the beneficiaries, all or part of this 35% tax can be reclaimed. This is a most attractive feature of such trusts.

For example, suppose that your father has set up an accumulation and maintenance trust of which the only beneficiary is your ten-year-old son Tom. For 1994–5 Tom has no other income and the trust pays £6,500 net for his maintenance and education. Income tax will be reclaimable as follows:

Gross income payment	10,000
Personal allowance	3,445
	6,555
Tax at 20% on £3,000	600.00
25% on £3,555	888.75
	1,488.75
Tax deducted from distribution	3,500.00
Income tax repayable	£2,011.25

6.14.2

The *capital gains tax* rules provide for a tax rate of 35%. However, as previously indicated, there is an annual exemption of normally half the amount applying for an individual.

1995–6
£3,000 Thus, the 1994–5 exemption for accumulation and maintenance settlements (and many other trusts) is £2,900. However, if you have created a number of settlements since 7 June 1978, the relief is proportionately reduced.

6.15 Tax Saving With Accumulation and Maintenance Trusts

Now for a few practical points about saving tax by creating accumulation and maintenance trusts for your children and grandchildren.

● Costs will be involved both in setting up the trust and in its ongoing administration, tax returns, etc. Thus you should be prepared to settle enough capital to make it worthwhile. £50,000 + would be the minimum.

- Although professional trustees are often used, you could normally be a trustee yourself. This enables you to keep tighter control over the trust assets.

- Remember that if you settle assets on your under-18 children, you will be assessed to tax on income distributed to them. The same applies to your spouse if he or she is the settlor. However, if your spouse has little or no income, it will not matter if he or she is assessed on distributions from the trust. So it would be better if your spouse is the settlor.

- Of course, grandparents make ideal settlors and will not be assessed on any income distributions made to minors. Also, they may have larger available funds than the parents. Furthermore, reducing their estates for inheritance tax purposes is more important at their stage in life.

- Nevertheless, as parents you can consider acting as the settlors, even if you both pay higher rate income tax. However, consider accumulating all of the income until the children come of age. Also, invest the funds in assets producing little or no income. Shares in your own company may well come into this category. Single premium life assurance bonds are another example.

- Although the children must obtain income as of right by age 25, their entitlement to the capital may be much later. In fact, the trust deed may leave the timing to the trustees at their discretion. You should seriously consider this feature for your own trust, since there is no knowing how early or late your children or grandchildren may become financially responsible.

- Because they are potentially exempt, transfers which you make into accumulation and maintenance settlements will not attract *inheritance tax*, unless you die within seven years. Also, as previously indicated, wide freedom is obtained from the tax within the trust and on distributions. This makes such trusts excellent for passing assets to your children or grandchildren without incurring inheritance tax.

- You need to watch the *capital gains tax* position. Assets that you settle will normally give rise to this tax as if you sold them for their market values. It thus makes sense to settle cash, gilts or other assets which are exempt from capital gains tax. Alternatively settle assets qualifying for gifts relief, such as shares in your family company, and make the appropriate hold-over election.

1995–6
£3,000 ● The trusts themselves produce a modest capital gains tax advantage in that they will each have an annual exemption of up to £2,900. Also, if you are a 40% tax payer, any gains realised by the trust will carry a slightly lower charge at 35%.

● The ongoing *income tax* savings are most valuable, especially if the settlor is not one of the parents of the beneficiaries. As seen, income distributions enable part or all of the accompanying 35% tax credit to be reclaimed. This makes accumulation and maintenance trusts excellent vehicles for paying school fees.

● Suppose you settle assets on your grandchildren, instead of your paying tax at, say, 40% on the income, the trust pays 35%. However, part or all of this will be reclaimable if the income is used for the education and maintenance of the beneficiaries.

6.16   Bare Trusts

If you do not wish to have an accumulation and maintenance trust for your minor child, an alternative is a bare trust. Such trusts are simpler and cheaper to administer. However, the scope is much narrower.

The settled property is held on a bare trust for the child. The income belongs to the child and is precluded from being accumulated by the trust deed. In practice, the trustees are likely to keep the income until the child attains his or her majority. This is because a minor cannot give a good receipt.

Since the income is taxed on the basis that it belongs to the child, there is no additional rate income tax to pay. Also, full relief is available for any unused personal allowance and lower rate band.

If you are the settlor and your child is the beneficiary, there is a risk that the income will be taxed as if it were your own for tax purposes. However, this can be avoided if the trust deed makes it clear that the income cannot be applied for your child's benefit.

Any capital gains are assessed on the beneficiary, who thus obtains the full £5,800 annual exemption. At 18, when the capital vests in the beneficiary, there is no capital gain. (The trust property forms part of the estate of the beneficiary for inheritance tax purposes.)

1995–6
£3,000

6.17 School Fees Arrangements

One of the main financial considerations regarding children is apt to be providing for their school fees. You should certainly aim to do so in the most tax-effective ways. Any arrangements that you make are also likely to be of use regarding higher education.

As previously indicated, trusts provide an ideal means of paying school fees. Income distributions are normally treated as belonging to the child for tax purposes. An exception is where parents are settlors and in other cases a worthwhile tax repayment is likely.

See 6.13

Accumulation and maintenance trusts and discretionary trusts can be used to provide students with the cost of their college fees and upkeep. Also, bare trusts can be used to provide funds at age 18 for these purposes.

Grandparents can play a vital part as the settlors of such trusts. As indicated earlier, this is normally more effective for tax purposes than where a parent is the settlor. Annual payments under deeds of covenant executed by grandparents before 15 March 1988 are also a tax-efficient way of contributing to school fees.

See 6.4

Otherwise, the grandparent could make annual gifts of capital within their £3,000 inheritance tax annual exemptions. This will have the effect of modestly reducing their estates without any exposure to inheritance tax on the gifts.

See 6.11

If you need to provide all or part of the cost of your children's education, various forms of investment might be considered. For example, personal equity plans (PEPs) carry freedom from income tax and capital gains tax, although there are management expenses.

You could invest up to the allowed £9,000 each year when the children are young. Hopefully, your PEPs will show healthy appreciation and you will realise them to pay school fees in future years.

Life assurance has long been a popular way of providing for school fees. However, the benefits were reduced when life assurance premium relief on new policies was removed (1984).

If you pay premiums on a qualifying life assurance policy (to continue for at least ten years) the proceeds will be tax free. You can then use them to fund school fees. An endowment policy would be suitable and, depending on its investment performance, this would work well.

Another form of life policy could be used at much shorter notice. This is the single premium policy or bond. The proceeds are taxable broadly at the excess of your top income tax rate over 25%. However, a particularly attractive feature is that no tax is immediately payable if your annual withdrawals are no more than 5%. Such withdrawals are ideal contributions towards school fees.

6.18   Planning List – Childhood

To conclude this chapter, here is a list of various tax-planning points which have been covered:

● Make use of the income tax allowances available to children.

● Employ your children in your business, if practicable.

● Use pre-15 March 1988 deeds of covenant.

● Consider whether your children might own suitable assets.

● Make use of capital gains tax reliefs available to children.

● Inheritance tax reliefs and nil rate band – use these in transfers to children.

● Make lifetime gifts for children.

- Consider the trusts which are suitable for children.

- Use accumulation and maintenance settlements for your children and grandchildren.

- Set up bare trusts for children.

- Make school fees arrangements:

  trusts
  PEPs
  qualifying life assurance policies
  single premium life policies.

CHAPTER SEVEN

Student Days

7.1

In his autobiography, Edward Gibbon, the famous historian, surprisingly wrote disparagingly about the time that he spend at Oxford. He said, 'I spent fourteen months at Magdalen college; they proved the fourteen months the most idle and unprofitable of my whole life.'

Nevertheless, many school leavers aspire to go to university or receive tertiary education in other ways. What is more, instead of Gibbon's 14 months, at least three years is the norm.

As in the childhood phase, students are likely to be at the receiving end of tax-planning arrangements. Your student children will need help with their college expenses and living costs. So probably you will make gifts and organise trust distributions where possible.

However, there are two important differences. Once a student reaches age 18, he or she attains majority and is able to own all kinds of property, including land. The other points is that a student would be a much more active participant than would a child. He or she would normally understand the arrangements and, furthermore, obtain wider financial experience from them.

7.2 Providing For Student Costs

Student costs consist mainly of fees, accommodation, food, clothes, books, travelling and recreation. These are likely to be covered in various ways.

Your local authority would normally cover the fees. Depending on your own and your spouse's income, and sometimes that of the student, there may also be grants and loans towards living expenses. The question is how to bridge the gap?

Holiday and other earnings of the student will certainly help. However, the student may be following a course which allows little time for employment. Also, holiday jobs may prove hard to get in times of recession. So you will need to step in. At least once the student has reached age 18, there is no danger of your being taxed on the income from any gifts or settlements that you make.

Apart from simply paying money when needed, the following is a selection of ways of providing for student costs which are dealt with in more detail later in this chapter and elsewhere:

Payments under pre-15 March 1988 deeds of covenant	*Refer to* *6.4*
Distributions from new or existing accumulation and maintenance trusts	*Refer to* *7.4*
Distributions from discretionary trusts	*Refer to* *7.5*
Bare trusts	*Refer to* *7.8.2*
PEPs owned by parents	*Refer to* *7.8*
Single premium and qualifying life policies on parents' lives	*Refer to* *7.8.1*
The outright ownership of accommodation by students	*Refer to* *7.9*
Investments held by students	*Refer to* *7.10*

NOTE Income from trusts, investments, properties and some deeds of covenant could reduce a student's grants towards living expenses. This needs watching, unless your income together with that of your spouse already exceed the limit.

7.3   The Student's Tax Benefits

Refer to 2.6–8 Remember that students have full allowances and tax rate scales. Thus, it is most beneficial for them to have their own income, so that their tax allowances are not wasted. This simply follows the general plan of spreading income within a family so as to reduce the overall tax cost.

1995–6
£3,525
£3,200
£21,100
 Any holiday and other earned income will be counted first. Thus, the first £3,445 will be tax free, the next £3,000 at 20% and the next £20,700 at 25%, before the 40% rate is reached.

As suggested for older children, if your student son or daughter needs employment, this could be with your family business. However, watch out for *national insurance contributions*. Once the weekly earnings reach £57, both the employers and student will have to make contributions.

See Appendix 16
1995–6
£58

Investment income will normally also attract tax reliefs and favourable tax rates. Thus, where the student has bank deposit and building society accounts, tax may be reclaimable in respect of the interest. However, if the income is likely to be covered by allowances, an election should be made to have it paid gross.

If the student is sufficiently responsible, gifts of shares and other investments can be made to him or her. The income will then be taxed at the more favourable rates likely to apply. An added bonus is that when the investments are sold by the student, his or her £5,800 annual capital gains tax exemption will be available.

1995–6
£6,000

See 6.13 Trusts provide the greatest flexibility and protection. But remember that as with investment income in general, income from trusts could result in the loss of means tested grants. However, families with spare funds for investments and trusts often would not qualify for any grants, apart from to cover the fees.

35% income tax may be suffered in the trust, which would normally apply for discretionary settlements and accumulation and maintenance ones. However, all or part of this tax may be reclaimable by beneficiaries receiving income distributions. Further details follow.

7.4 Accumulation and Maintenance Trusts for Students

Accumulation and maintenance settlements are considered in the previous chapter. Whether or not they have been established before the beneficiaries reach the student stage, they are ideal for providing income for paying college expenses.

See 6.14

This is so, even if you are both the father and the settlor. Once the beneficiaries reach their eighteenth birthdays, you will no longer be assessed to tax on any income distributed to them.

Similarly, once your children reach their majorities, whether or not they are students, there is no reason why you should not establish an accumulation and maintenance settlement for them. Of course, no one can be included as a beneficiary if he or she has passed age 25. This is because by that age, beneficiaries need to have a share of the income as of right.

Once the beneficiaries do have such a right to income as previously explained, they do not need to obtain capital. This can be left to a later age stated in the trust deed. Indeed, the matter can be left entirely to the trustees, who could be you and your spouse.

Thus, if you do not consider a beneficiary to be sufficiently mature, you could defer releasing the capital and simply pay income to him or her. However, if you require a more flexible arrangement, a discretionary settlement should be considered.

7.5 Discretionary Settlements

Discretionary settlements are those where the application of the income and capital is left to the discretion of the trustees. You may be a trustee yourself. Otherwise, it would be usual for you to give a letter of wishes to the trustees. This would state in broad terms how you would wish the trust assets and income to be handled, particularly in the event of your death.

The income is taxed according to the rules for trusts with no interests in possession. These are as described for accumulation and maintenance settlements in the previous chapter. Similarly, the capital gains tax rules are broadly the same as for such trusts.

However, there is one important advantage regarding settling assets on discretionary trusts. Full capital gains tax gifts hold-over relief is available, provided you make the required election to the Revenue.

Where assets are settled into other types of trust, gifts relief is only available in certain cases. Particular examples are assets used in your business and shares in family trading companies.

Also see
3.34 The *inheritance tax* rules for discretionary settlements are completely different from those applying to other types and need to be carefully watched. Transfers into and out of discretionary settlements are chargeable transfers and are not potentially exempt. Furthermore, the trust assets are charged to inheritance tax every ten years, subject to the rules.

Fortunately, special rates apply when you make transfers into a discretionary trust. These rates cover funds originally settled and subsequent additions.

1995–6
£154,000 The rate is half the normal 40%. However, this 20% so-called lifetime rate only applies after your £150,000 nil rate band has been used up. For this purpose, you must consider other chargeable transfers (not PETs) during the last seven years. However, if you should die within seven years of a PET, the original inheritance tax may need revising.

If you settle all or part of your shares in an unquoted trading company,
Also see the effect of *business property relief* is striking. If your initial holding exceeds
3.32.5 25%, relief of 100% is obtained. Thus, no inheritance tax is normally payable and no inroads are made into your nil rate band. Where your initial holding is no more than 25%, your relief is restricted to 50%.

You should note that business property relief will be available, subject to the rules, regarding the ten-year and exit charges. But you may find that, although you qualified for 100% relief, the trust's holding only attracts 50%. The detailed rules for the relief must be borne in mind, especially that it may be lost if the assets are disposed of.

The ten-year charge is only at 30% of the lifetime rate. This means 30%

122

of 20%, or 6%. Furthermore, the tax is charged on the assets held on discretionary trusts and, if these are worth less than the £150,000 nil rate band, none normally arises.

If any assets are held for less than the full ten-year period, a reduction is made in the tax on those assets. The fraction N/40ths is used, where N is the number of completed periods of three months for which the assets have been held on discretionary trusts during the ten-year period.

Where capital is distributed to beneficiaries, 'exit charges' arise. These are calculated on the same basis as the ten-year charges. The N/40 fraction must be applied, defined as above. Thus, if capital is distributed five years after the last ten-year anniversary, the full tax would be reduced by one half. The exit and ten-year charges are illustrated in the following example.

7.6 Example: Discretionary Settlements – Inheritance Tax

Mary established a wholly discretionary settlement on 1 January 1993 with property worth £200,000. In the previous seven years, she had made chargeable transfer of £100,000.

The settlement distributes capital of £50,000 on 15 March 1998. Assume that inheritance tax rates remain at the 1994–5 levels and there are no more capital distributions. Assume also that the trust property remains 'relevant property' (broadly entirely on discretionary trusts).

Taking the property value on 1 January 2003 as £400,000, the exit charge and ten-year charge will be:

Exit charge at 15 March 1998

Value of property when settled	£200,000	
Chargeable transfers made by settlor in seven years before commencement	100,000	(A)
	£300,000	(B)

Inheritance tax on (B)	£150,000 at nil	–	
	150,000 at 40%	£60,000	

Lifetime inheritance tax 50%	30,000
Less notional inheritance tax on (A) at nil	–
	£30,000

The effective rate is 30,000/200,000	15%
Number of completed three-month periods prior to the distribution	20
Thus the inheritance tax on the distribution of £50,000 is 30% × £50,000 × 15% × 20/40 =	£1,125

Ten-year charge at 1 January 2003

Value of property	£400,000	
Pre-settlement transfers	100,000	(A)
	£500,000	(C)

Inheritance tax on (C)	£150,000 at nil	–
	£350,000 at 40%	£140,000

Lifetime inheritance tax 50% × £140,000	£70,000
Less notional inheritance tax on (A) at nil	–
	£70,000
Ten-year charge 30% × £70,000	£21,000

7.7 Using Discretionary Settlements to Provide For Students

Discretionary settlements are ideal for passing income on to students to cover their study and living expense costs. As mentioned, this facilitates substantial income tax repayment claims. For this reason, it is generally better to make distributions of income, rather than capital.

One advantage of discretionary trusts is that income can be passed to different beneficiaries at different times. For example, suppose brothers Tom, Dick and Harry are beneficiaries and they each go to university, then obtain well-paid jobs.

Tom is the oldest and when he goes to university, the trust pays him £10,000 for three years. After that, his salary is too high for much tax to be reclaimed. After that, Dick receives trust income distributions for his college expenses, later followed by Harry. In this example, the trust pays out a steady stream of income and, eventually, rough parity between the brothers should be attained.

Remember that trust tax benefits are not lost if income remains undistributed for some years. When the accumulated income is later distributed, the 35% tax credit remains available. Depending on the tax position of the recipient, it can be wholly or partly repaid.

There may be circumstances when large income payments to students should be considered, much higher than their immediate needs. This is because students generally have little or no other income. Thus, their income tax allowances and lower income tax bands are likely to be almost intact. This makes them ideal recipients of large income distributions, at least from a tax viewpoint.

Thus, suppose that for 1994–5 Susan has no other income. A gross income distribution of £27,000 attracts no more than 25% income tax in her hands. This compares with 35% in the trust. Taking account of her £3,445 personal allowance, her tax is £5,738.75 and £3,711.25 is reclaimable. The money available for her is:

Gross distribution	£27,000.00
Less 35% withheld	9,450.00
	17,550.00
Income tax repayment	3,711.25
Available for Susan	£21,261.25

Of course, it would make sense for there to be an understanding as to how Susan uses the money. Any excess over her normal expenses should perhaps be invested by her.

Also see 6.17 ## 7.8   Ongoing Educational Arrangements

As mentioned in the previous chapter, school fees schemes generally need some years to become worthwhile. The underlying investments take time to grow. It is thus seldom sensible to start such schemes for paying university expenses once the student has come of age.

However, it may well be that arrangements are already in place and investments have not been wholly used up on school fees. Thus, you may have been investing in PEPs to pay school fees and some remain. These can be used towards your children's expenses concerning their further education.

You can, of course, continue to build up your PEPs to the annual limits of £9,000 for each of yourself and your spouse. As for the students themselves investing in PEPs, this will not normally be tax efficient, since they would be unlikely to pay very much tax. The result would be that the management expenses of the PEPs would outweigh the tax savings.

7.8.1

Single premium life assurance bonds may have been bought to fund school fees and you could have some left over. If you are a higher rate income tax payer, do not cash them yourself, since this would involve extra tax.

Better gift the bonds to your children, which will involve you in no income tax or capital gains tax. Assuming that they would not be liable to higher rate tax, they will pay no extra tax on realising the bonds.

7.8.2

Also see 6.16 *Bare trusts* have been suggested as a means of building up capital funds available for when your children come of age. To obtain the best effect, this should be arranged as early as possible. In this way the income can accumulate and the tax be reclaimed as appropriate.

The children will thus have money to fund their higher education exactly when needed. However, they will need to be trustworthy regarding the proper use of the money. If any of your children is insufficiently mature and you feel unable to trust them with large sums of money, another method should be considered. For example, an accumulation and maintenance settlement may fit the bill.

7.9   Living Accommodation

Students need somewhere to live when they are at university. Sometimes they will live in hall, so that no particular planning is needed. However, often at least part of their university years will be spent in 'digs', that is to say rented houses or flats.

Instead of paying rent, it may be better if you or your student son or daughter owns the accommodation. Certainly there is the chance of capital appreciation between when it is bought and sold. Also, it may prove cheaper in the long run to own rather than rent.

Often, the property will be too large for just one. Then, a sensible arrange- *See* ment would be to let the spare rooms to other students. Of course, the *2.16.4* rents less expenses will be taxable, but if the income belongs to the student, it may well be within his or her personal relief.

Furthermore, the student may well be able to benefit from the 'rent-a- *See* room' relief. If the house or flat is his or her main residence and the rent *2.16.5* is less than £3,250 for a year, no income tax is normally payable. Otherwise, limited relief may be available. An election can be made to be taxed on the excess of the gross rents over £3,250, with no deduction for expenses.

Suppose you buy the property yourself and let your student son or daughter live there. If, at the same time, you charge rent to other occupants, you will be taxed without the benefit of 'rent-a-room' relief. However, any mortgage interest that you pay on a loan taken to buy the property can be offset against the net rents and thus obtain tax relief.

If your student son or daughter borrows money to buy a property as a main residence, tax relief is limited to 20% (15% from 1995–6). What is *See* more, the bank or building society are likely to require you to provide a *2.12–13* guarantee for the loan. Another advantage of the student owning the property as his or her main residence is the availability of capital gains tax exemption.

You will observe that there are many factors to consider. The best tax results are likely where the student owns the property and uses it as his or her main residence. Then there will normally be a substantial amount of tax relief. However, you will need to be able to afford to gift the property to the student. Alternatively, you might guarantee a loan for its purchase.

In rare cases, the student may already have funds to purchase a property, such as resulting from a large trust distribution. Rather than distributing trust funds, it is worth considering whether the settlement should not buy the property. An advantage is that it has not permanently parted with the funds. Also, if the student makes the property his or her main residence, capital gains tax relief is available.

In spite of the extra tax breaks from your student son or daughter owning the property, you may prefer to do so. Indeed, it may prove a profitable short-term investment.

See 3.2 et seq Furthermore, when you sell, you will have the benefit of indexation relief and unused annual exemption before paying any capital gains tax. Also, the ability to set interest on any loan you took to buy the property against your rental income provides further valuable tax relief.

Thus, whoever is to own the property, there is much to be said in favour of purchasing it. However, it is essential that the property is worth buying from an investment point of view. It is no good buying a house or flat on which you are likely to lose money on its resale.

7.10　Investments Held By Students

Throughout this chapter, various references have been made to investments being put into the hands of students. These include bank and building society deposit accounts, equities and single premium life assurance bonds.

Certainly, where students have their own investments, the income is often free of income tax or taxed at lower rates, because they have unused allowances. At the same time, it is a favourable position regarding capital taxes, where the younger members of a family own assets.

As well as investments already mentioned, savings bonds should be considered. You might arrange with your student son or daughter that the units should only be encashed with your agreement and you might take charge thereof.

Another form of investment which may be appropriate to pass to your student children is an interest in your family trading company. As explained elsewhere, capital gains tax hold-over relief and inheritance tax business property relief are normally available.   *See 8.8*

In order to be more selective regarding paying dividends to your student children, they might be given a special class of shares. Special dividends could then be paid only on these shares. Alternatively, dividend waivers might be used to pay the students a bigger proportion of the dividends, if appropriate.

7.11   Planning List – Student Days

- Make full use of income tax allowances and rates, but be careful of the effect of extra income on *student grants*.

- Fully use capital gains tax exemptions.

- Make payments to students under pre-15 March 1988 deeds of covenant.

- Use discretionary trusts to distribute income and capital to students.

- Distribute income to students from existing or newly created accumulation and maintenance settlements.

- Use a bare trust to provide funds when a student comes of age.

- Gift single premium life assurance bonds to your student children so that they can encash them.

- Buy accommodation for your children to occupy when at university.

- Help your student children to own property where they reside whilst at university by, for example, outright gift or guaranteeing loans for them to buy.

- Make gifts to students of shares and other investments.

CHAPTER EIGHT

Early Working Life

8.1

For all that, in the words attributed to Oscar Wilde, 'Work is the curse of the drinking classes', most young people aspire to it. Often starting from humble beginnings, progress may be rapid, but seldom as startlingly so as with Sir Joseph Porter in Gilbert and Sullivan's *HMS Pinafore*, who explained:

> When I was a lad I served a term
> as office boy to an Attorney's firm.
> I cleaned the windows and I swept the floor,
> And I polished up the handle of the big front door.
> I polished up the handle so carefully
> That now I am the Ruler of the Queen's Navy.

This chapter covers tax planning during the first ten years or so of your working life. Among the matters considered are:

	Refer to:
Pension arrangements	*8.2, 8.6.1 & 8.12*
Company cars	*8.3*
Interest-free loans	*8.4.1*
Private sickness insurance	*8.4.2*
Profit-related pay schemes	*8.4.3*
Share option schemes	*8.4.4*
Employee share ownership plans (ESOPS)	*8.4.4*
Working overseas	*8.5*
Becoming a director	*8.7*
Capital tax reliefs regarding family company shares	*8.8*

The exact details will largely depend on the course which your career takes. To help illustrate some of the various possibilities, the careers of three different people are considered; Tom, Dick and Harry.

Tom obtains a professional qualification and works conscientiously as an employee, steadily progressing.

Dick is an able young man. He is fortunate in that he enjoys working in the flourishing manufacturing business set up by his father.

Harry is a bright entrepreneur who is left money in his aunt's will. This enables him to go into business on his own.

8.2   Tax Planning For Tom

8.2.1

Tom's tax planning will much depend on what his employers are willing to provide. Perhaps the most valuable 'perk' is a really good *pension scheme*.

If Tom belongs to his company's pension scheme, his employers will be required to contribute to it. In addition, if the scheme is contributory, Tom will make contributions himself. Provided the scheme is approved by the Inland Revenue and the contributions are within certain limits, they will attract full tax relief.

Most company schemes are granted what is known as *exempt approval*. That results in your own and your employers' contributions not only obtaining full tax relief, but also accumulating in a fund which is normally free of income tax and capital gains tax. The following are some of the main features that a company scheme like Tom's is likely to have:

● Pensions commence between 60 and 75 years of age. Earlier retirement is often allowed at any age due to illness and otherwise no earlier than 50.

● Either the pension is calculated on a final salary basis or there is a money purchase scheme. Subject to commuting part for a lump sum (s below), Tom will be taxed on his pension.

- Under the final salary basis, pension is calculated as a fraction of final salary, typically $\frac{1}{60}$th for each year of service up to a maximum of 40. This gives a maximum pension of two-thirds of final salary. However, the Revenue may allow the maximum pension after a shorter period of service.

- In a money purchase scheme, subject to Revenue limits, Tom's pension would be related to the value of the fund created from his contributions, rather than his final remuneration.

- Should Tom die in service, a lump sum of up to four times his final remuneration can be paid tax free to his widow or other beneficiaries. If he dies after retirement, the scheme can provide for his widow to receive a pension of up to two-thirds of his own.

- On retirement, Tom will be able to commute part of his pension and receive a tax-free lump sum instead. This is tax-efficient since even if extra pension is required, this can be provided by a purchased annuity which will include a tax-free portion representing repayments of capital. The normal pension from the scheme would be fully taxable. *Also see 12.2*

- The lump sum is in general limited to the greater of $\frac{3}{80}$ths of final remuneration for each of the first 40 years of service and $2\frac{1}{4}$ times the non-commuted pension. If Tom's final remuneration is over £100,000, it is 'capped' at this level for these purposes. (The Revenue often allow maximum commutation to be available after a shorter period of service.)

8.2.2

If Tom does not wish to join his company scheme, or if there is none, he can subscribe to one or more *personal pension schemes*. The details are shown later, in the section dealing with Harry. However, one particular feature is that, as an employee, Tom would normally pay his contributions net of basic rate income tax. *See 8.12*

As Tom progresses and his salary grows, he should seek to maximise his pension contributions. On the basis that his company scheme is contributory, his own contributions can be up to 15% of his remuneration. If the 15% is not fully used, he can put the balance into an additional voluntary contribution (AVC) scheme provided by his employers.

Alternatively, Tom can use a free-standing additional voluntary contribution (FSAVC) scheme, which is independent of his employers.

8.3 A Company Car For Tom?

Also see 2.17.6–7 Until recently, there would have been little doubt of the value of a company car as a tax saving 'perk'. However, scale charges have steadily increased and employer's national insurance contributions have been imposed. As a result, the tax costs of company cars are more for both employers and employees.

In spite of this, there is a fair chance that Tom will be better off having his car provided by his employers, rather than having a higher salary and buying it himself. This is certainly likely if his annual business mileage exceeds 18,000, so that the 35% scale charge is discounted by two-thirds.

If Tom's annual business mileage is between 2,500 and 18,000, the benefit of having a company car is less and may be wiped out altogether by the tax. For example, suppose his car cost £10,000. The corresponding taxable amount is 35% (£3,500) less one-third discount, giving £2,333.

Suppose that the annual depreciation is £2,000 and that the employers pay all of the expenses (but not necessarily petrol). The annual value of the benefit of their providing Tom with a car would be, say:

Depreciation	2,000
Repairs and servicing	500
Road tax	130
Insurance	450
	£3,080

£135 from 30.11.94 (note beside Road tax / Insurance)

Thus he would be receiving over £3,000-worth of remuneration and be taxed on only £2,333.

The position regarding the employers paying for Tom's private petrol is that this would only make sense if he does sufficient private mileage each year. Assuming his car is in the 1401–2000cc band, the scale charge for 1994–5 would be £810. Taking 25 miles per gallon, and a cost of £2 per gallon, he would need private mileage of over 10,000 to break even.

8.4 Other 'Perks' For Tom

The range of 'perks' which are provided for Tom is entirely at the discretion of his employers, so he will be able to do no more than make suggestions. However, he will be in a better bargaining position when he negotiates his remuneration packet on changing jobs. Examples are given below.

8.4.1

Interest free loans are now only taxed if their total amount exceeds £5,000. Thus Tom could be given such loans by his employers up to that amount. A usual purpose would be to buy rail season tickets. Larger loans are taxed on the basis of the 'official rate', which is 8.0% from 6 November 1994. But even that is a lower rate than Tom would be likely to pay.

8.4.2

Private sickness insurance is a highly valuable perk for Tom to have. He will be taxed on any premiums paid by his employers. However, by participating in their group scheme, the cost is likely to be much less than if he had arranged it himself.

8.4.3

If his employers have a *profit related pay* (PRP) scheme, it will be to his advantage to belong. This will result in 20% of his yearly PAYE pay being free of tax, with a maximum relief of £4,000. If he pays 40% tax, the maximum relief in terms of tax is £1,600.

135

8.4.4

As Tom progresses, he may be invited to join a *share option scheme* operated by his company. Under the 1984 rules, he is entitled to have options over shares with a specified maximum value at the time of grant. This maximum is the greater of £100,000 and four times his current year's emoluments (or those for the previous year if larger).

Subject to certain rules, any gains made by Tom will only be subject to capital gains tax and not income tax, as would be the case with some non-approved schemes. Thus the benefits of indexation relief and any unused annual exemption would apply.

Other tax effective share arrangements are available, including certain profit sharing schemes and employee share ownership plans (ESOPs). What really matters is how the actual employer company's shares perform and the results can be spectacular.

Also see
10.11
8.5 Tom Works Overseas For a Period

Part of Tom's natural career progression could well include spending a period working overseas. This might come about through his being posted there by his present employers. Alternatively, he could change jobs, taking a new one overseas.

Provided the level of taxes is lower in his new country of work than here, tax savings are to be expected. In addition, rates of pay are likely to be more and so he should be able to return home at the end of his assignment with a healthy capital sum.

Tom should select an assignment which keeps him out of the UK long enough for him to be neither resident nor ordinarily resident here for tax purposes. This will normally result in his overseas earnings being free of UK tax. Furthermore, he generally will be free of capital gains tax on his disposals during the period.

See
2.21.2–
3
In order for Tom to be treated as neither resident nor ordinarily resident for the term he spends abroad under his contract, he will need to meet the following conditions:

- Either all his duties are performed abroad or any performed here are only incidental to his overseas duties.

- His absence from the UK and his employment abroad must last for at least a whole tax year.

- During his absence, Tom must not spend more than 182 days in the UK in any tax year.

- His periods in the UK must also not exceed an average of 91 days a tax year, taken over the period of absence with a maximum of 4 years.

Subject to the above, Tom will be treated as neither resident nor ordinarily resident from the day he leaves the UK until the day of his return. He will then be ready to meet the next stage of his life with valuable experience gained abroad and hopefully a healthy capital sum.

8.6   Tax Planning For Dick

Most of the benefits already mentioned as being applicable for Tom will apply also to Dick. However, working in the family business, he should be in a much better position to obtain them.

Assuming that he has a good working relationship with his father, it would make sense for his remuneration package to include tax-efficient items such as pension scheme membership and share option scheme participation. Also, if his business mileage is sufficient, a company car is indicated.

See 8.2, 8.3 & 8.4.4

8.6.1

Dick's pension arrangements may be provided by a *self-administered scheme*, effectively run by the company. If this also covers his father and other key employees, the pension scheme will be able to build up a substantial fund. This can be used to buy property for use by the company. Also, subject to the rules, the fund can lend money to the company.

A self-administered scheme must have a 'pensioneer trustee', usually an actuary. The trustees of a small self-administered scheme have wide investment powers, subject to some Inland Revenue conditions. In particular, investments must be commercial and any dealings with the company, its shareholders or directors should be on an arm's-length basis.

Property can be bought from and/or leased back to the company. Also, money can be borrowed to finance purchases of property, subject to a limit of three times the ordinary annual scheme contributions. Loans back to the company are normally limited to 25% of the scheme contributions for the first two years of the scheme and 50% thereafter. Such loans must be on a commercial arm's length basis.

8.7   Dick Becomes a Director

Dick progresses well and before many years have passed, he becomes a director of the family company. The taxation effects of this development will not be dramatic. However, Dick will take on a higher profile as regards the Inland Revenue.

One area where there are certain special rules for directors is pensions. If Dick controls less than 20% of the shares of his company, his final salary for pension purposes will be calculated on a less favourable basis. Choosing the best year from the last five will not be allowed.

In some cases, Dick will not be allowed to belong at all to the pension scheme of a family investment company. In particular, he would be excluded if he controls at least 20% of the shares and over 50%, together with his family (father, etc.).

Also see 11.4 ## 8.8   Passing Family Company Shares to Dick

When it becomes clear that Dick will stay with the company, arrangements should be made for him to obtain its shares. He could buy some from his father or other shareholders. Alternatively, his father or perhaps mother might give him some. Another possibility is that shares could be settled for the benefit of himself and other members of the family.

The tax treatment of gifts is most favourable. So far as capital gains tax is concerned, the normal basis would be to tax the excess of the market value over the cost, allowing for indexation and the annual exemption.

138

However, it will be open to Dick and the donor (his father, etc.) to elect for the gain to be held over. Unquoted trading company shares is one of the categories of assets for which this election can be made.

If the shares are sold to Dick by, say, his father, any shortfall of the price compared with the true value could be treated as a gift for tax purposes.

Should Dick's father have reached age 60 (or retires younger because of ill health) generous capital gains tax retirement relief will be available. Gains up to £250,000 are relieved in full with 50% from £250,000 to £1,000,000. *See 3.21.6*

The inheritance tax position is even more favourable. Provided the parents have more than 25% of the votes, they obtain 100% business property relief on gifting the shares. That means that the gifts are not even treated as potentially exempt. With smaller holdings, 50% relief is obtained. However, in that situation, the annual exemption (£3,000) and nil rate band (£150,000) are likely to come into play. *See 3.32.5*

1995–6 £154,000

Business property relief makes it particularly attractive to settle shares into a discretionary trust. If 100% relief is available, no inheritance tax will be payable at that stage. Of course, as in other cases, the relief could be lost if the donor dies within seven years of the gift, before which time the shares have been disposed of.

As can be seen, the gifts reliefs available at present are highly favourable. However, these cannot be guaranteed to last for ever and if the Government changes, they might be withdrawn or made less favourable. So it would make sense for Dick's parents to act reasonably soon.

Another way for Dick to obtain an interest in the business would be for him to form his own new company. This can undertake new but related activities. In this way, the new company can be built up and will become more valuable, perhaps at the expense of the old one. This method was more popular when the business property reliefs were lower and it should be taken into account, should those reliefs be reduced.

8.9 Tax Planning For Harry

Harry starts business as a sole trader, operating from home. He should claim a proportion of the expenses of his home against the business. However, he should not claim that any rooms are used exclusively for business purposes in case capital gains tax main residence relief is impeded.

So far as using a car for business is concerned, there are no quandaries about claiming relief for income tax purposes. This should certainly be done. Normally petrol, oil, repairs, car tax and insurance will all be allowable, subject to a proportional disallowance for personal use. In addition, capital allowances will be available, normally subject to the same disallowance.

8.10   VAT on Harry's Car Expenses

A word about VAT would be appropriate here. In general, Harry will need to register for VAT if his annual turnover exceeds £45,000. However, he could apply for voluntary registration below that level and that would allow him relief for the tax on his purchases (input tax).

£46,000 from 30.11.94

If registered, he needs to choose whether or not to claim input tax relief on his car expenses. Should he do so, he will be charged VAT on a quarterly or monthly scale which is intended to cover the personal use. (If there is no such use, the scale does not apply.)

1995–6

£167 £151
£195 £212
£315

Supposing his car's capacity is 1400cc or less, the quarterly charge would be £160 if petrol driven and £145 if diesel. The diesel figure increases to £187 above 2000cc, whilst for petrol driven cars, £202 applies above 1400cc and £300 above 2000cc.

Thus Harry should only charge his business and personal car expenses for VAT purposes if they are in excess of the appropriate scale figure. Otherwise he should notify the VAT office that he will not be claiming input tax relief on his car expenses.

8.11   How Harry's New Business is Taxed

Harry is starting his business under the new current year assessment scheme. As a result, his scope for tax planning is somewhat less than under the old, previous year system. However, much can still be done.

The regular ongoing basis of assessment is on the profits for the accounts year ending in the year of assessment. Thus, Harry could prepare accounts ended on any date from 6 April 1995 to 5 April 1996 and still be assessed on them for 1995–6.

See 2.18.2

What is more, the tax would be payable at the same times. Thus it would be of benefit for Harry to prepare his annual accounts to a date near the start of the tax year. In this way he will have longer to pay the tax.

When Harry commences trading, he will be assessed for the tax year in which he starts on the profits for that tax year. The assessment for the second tax year normally will be on the first year's profits and after that, the regular ongoing basis generally will apply.

For example, suppose he commences on 6 June 1995 and his profits for the year to 5 June 1996 are £24,000 and those to 5 June 1997 are £26,000. His assessments will be:

1995–6 (10 months to 5 April 1996 $\frac{10}{12}$ × £24,000)	£20,000
1996–7 (first complete accounts year)	£24,000
1997–8 (year ending within tax year)	£26,000

Note that Harry will be assessed on a good part of his first year's profits twice. Thus if he can reduce these subject to the rules, he may save extra tax. For example, he might defer finalising a sales contract until the next year, or incur extra expenses in the opening one.

Instead of making a profit in his first year, Harry could well make a loss. It would then be open to him to claim relief against other income assessed in the three previous years. (Similar relief applies for the next three years.) Any remaining loss could be offset against other income of the current year and the balance carried forward against income from the trade.

8.12   Pension Arrangements For Harry

As soon as he is making profits and he can afford it, Harry should consider starting pension arrangements for himself. The earlier he does so, the longer will the funds have to grow. Since he is self-employed, he will need to use personal pension plans. Subject to given limits, he will then obtain full tax relief for his contributions and they will accumulate in a tax-free fund.

The limits are expressed as percentages of the earnings assessed for the tax year when the contributions are paid as follows:

Age at start of tax year	% of net relevant earnings
Under 36	17.5
36–45	20
46–50	25
51–55	30
56–60	35
61 and over	40

1995–6
£78,600 'Net relevant earnings' are arrived at after making certain deductions such as capital allowances. They are subject to a 'cap' of currently £76,800, so that the maximum relief is calculated on this amount.

Special rules enable Harry to carry back contributions to the previous tax year, provided the available relief had not fully been used. Also, unused relief can be carried forward for up to six years, so that it can be used in making contributions in those later years.

Also see 8.13   Should Harry Incorporate?
10.10

Harry's business flourishes. He moves into separate business premises and takes on more and more staff. His profits grow rapidly and the question arises, should he now trade through a company?

1995–6
£24,300 Certainly, so far as income tax is concerned, it may well make sense. Once his profits clear of allowances exceed £23,700 for 1994–5, Harry will pay income tax of 40% on the excess. However, if he formed a company, it would only pay corporation tax at 25% until its profits became substantial.

142

In fact, if Harry had no other companies, he could make profits of up to £300,000 subject to the small companies rate of 25%. Only above that level would the full rate of 33% be phased in.

See 2.24

Of course, if Harry draws money out of the company as director's remuneration, it will bear tax at his full income tax rates. However, there will be scope for him to limit his income so that he pays no more than the basic rate. (Any dividends taken will result in him paying 20% in addition to the tax credit, once he is in the higher rate range. This is because dividends only carry a 20% tax credit against higher rate tax.)

For example, suppose that Harry has formed a company and the only tax relief that he is entitled is the personal allowance (£3,445). He would pay higher rate at £23,700 + £3,445 = £27,145. Thus, assuming he has no other income, he could limit his remuneration from the company for the tax year to £27,145. In this way, he would avoid paying higher rate income tax for that year.

1995–6
£3,525

1995–6
£27,825

Against the income tax savings from incorporating must be weighed the extra cost of National Insurance contributions. As a self-employed person, Harry will be paying Class 2 contributions of £5.65 each week and Class 4 of 7.3% on his earnings in the £6,340 to £21,840 band. What is more, half of the Class 4 contributions are deductible for income tax purposes.

See Appendix 16

1995–6
See 4.15

Operating through a company, contributions will only be payable on his remuneration, but at higher rates. Both the company and himself will be liable for Class 1 contributions on his earnings.

The company pays on the entire remuneration without limit at 10.2%. (This assumes he is not contracted-out.) However, the company deducts its contributions in arriving at its taxable profits.

Harry gets no tax relief for his own Class 1 contributions. These are paid on his earnings up to £430 per week (£22,360 annually) at 2% for the first £57 and the rest at 10%. (A graduated scale applies at lower levels.)

1995–6
£440
£58

The comparison does not only depend on how much money is being made by the business, but also what remuneration Harry draws from the company. However, if self-employed, there is clearly an earnings ceiling of £21,840, above which he pays no further contributions.

1995–6
£22,880

The comparable ceiling regarding his company remuneration is £22,360, but the company goes on paying at 10.2% without limit. Bearing in mind that at that level, Harry will soon be paying higher rate, little further net savings will result from increasing his remuneration.

To sum up, worthwhile tax advantages will only be gained from incorporation when Harry's profits put him into the higher rate income tax band. At that stage, larger net tax savings will result where he limits his annual remuneration.

However, one important factor to consider is that much higher pension contributions are possible using a company scheme. Also, commercial aspects, such as the benefits of a company's limited liability, are of paramount importance.

8.14　Planning List – Early Working Life

● Join your company pension scheme or have personal pension arrangements.

● Consider self-administered pension schemes if it is your decision.

● Carefully examine whether you should have a company car, since they are not always tax-efficient.

● Benefit from interest free loans, which are useful perks, particularly where within the £5,000 tax-free band.

● Participate in profit related pay schemes, since these result in useful tax savings.

● Make share option schemes available for senior staff as appropriate, since these can result in large profits.

● Investigate using employee share ownership plans (ESOPS), which are worthwhile arrangements with a tax-saving element.

● Maximise the tax-saving opportunities arising from a period of work overseas.

● Make sure that the valuable inheritance tax and capital gains tax reliefs are used when shares in your family company are passed down to you.

● As a sole trader, make full use of the tax planning opportunities arising in your opening years of trading.

● Watch the VAT on car expenses and carefully consider whether you should not opt out.

● Take account of the balance between tax and National Insurance contributions and other factors before incorporating a successful business.

CHAPTER NINE

Newly Married

9.1

In the previous chapter, we traced the early careers of Tom, Dick and Harry, as they took their different paths. But sooner or later, they may well all follow suit and get married. After all, in the words of Samuel Johnson: 'Marriage has many pains but celibacy has no pleasures.'

However, Dr Johnson also sounded a cautious note when he said: 'Now that you are going to marry, do not expect more from life than life will afford.'

He was not speaking only about the financial side, but his advice certainly holds good in that context. Fortunately, there are many opportunities for tax saving at the time of marriage and subsequently. These will certainly help to maximise after-tax income and thus increase what can be afforded.

This chapter deals with tax planning related to the newly wed, including what parents and grandparents can do. Topics covered include:

Refer to:

9.2	Inheritance tax marriage gift exemptions
9.3	Purchasing your home
9.4	Arranging your mortgage
9.6	Maximising the benefits of separate taxation
9.8	Joint investment and mortgage elections
9.9	Employing your spouse
9.11	Entering into partnership with your spouse

9.2   Inheritance Tax Marriage Gifts Exemptions

When you marry, the opportunity arises for the parents and grandparents on both sides to make gifts and settlements. These can be covered wholly or partly by the special inheritance tax marriage exemptions. Often, it will be worthwhile to exceed these, since there may be unused annual exemptions and the nil rate band.

The inheritance tax marriage exemptions apply to gifts in consideration of marriage. This broadly means made on the occasion of a marriage and conditional on it taking place. The exemption limits per donor are:

£5,000 if the donor is a parent of one of the marriage partners.

£2,500 for gifts from each grandparent and great-grandparent of the bride and groom.

£1,000 each for gifts from anyone else.

Of course, any gifts that you make in excess of your exemptions will be PETs. Thus they will only come into the reckoning for inheritance tax purposes if you die within seven years. For this reason, the reliefs for gifts from the grandparents are generally more important than those relating to the parents.   *See 3.24*

However, in the case of gifts that would otherwise carry the lifetime rate of 20%, the exemptions are particularly valuable. In particular, this would apply to discretionary settlements.

For example, suppose your daughter is getting married and you have used none of your £3,000 annual exemption for the current tax year or the previous one. You will have exemptions available amounting to 2 × £3,000 (annual exemption) and £5,000 marriage exemption, making £11,000 in all.

Using your nil rate band of £150,000, you will be able to put up to £161,000 into a discretionary settlement without paying any inheritance   *1995–6 £154,000*

147

tax. The beneficiaries should include your daughter and perhaps son-in-law, along with any future offspring. You could also give the trustees power to add additional beneficiaries.

If you wish to pass down even more funds at this stage, your spouse might also set up a discretionary settlement in this way.

Over and above the special exemptions, the marriage of a child provides a good opportunity for you both to reduce your estates for inheritance tax purposes. Naturally, this assumes that you can afford it.

When it comes to substantial inheritance tax planning, it is often difficult to take the plunge, even though the benefits might be enormous. So why not treat the wedding of your child or grandchild as a spur to action?

9.3   The Purchase of Your Home

The most important financial matter that is likely to occupy you in your early married life is the purchase of a house or flat. This presupposes that you choose to buy rather than rent. A few years ago, that certainly seemed to be the right answer, since house prices had generally risen, sometimes steeply. But the subsequent fall in house prices cast some doubt.

However, over the years, prices seem likely to rise, especially taking account of inflation. Furthermore, if you merely rent your home, it never becomes your own, whilst if you buy it, you acquire a worthwhile asset. Thus, on balance, it appears better to buy.

You should carefully consider purchasing the home in your joint names. This has much to recommend it. For inheritance tax purposes, it is generally advantageous to split your assets between you. For example, it enables you each to make gifts to your heirs, as appropriate. For income tax purposes, there is greater flexibility regarding mortgage interest, as is shown later.

You should discuss with your solicitor how he will structure the joint ownership of the house. This can either be as joint tenants or tenants in common.

Under a joint tenancy, the share of the first of you to die passes to the survivor. This is useful from the point of view of his or her security. However, neither of you will be able to dispose of your respective share by gift or will, which hampers inheritance tax planning.

For tax planning purposes, it is better to own the house as tenants in common. In this way, you will each have a clearly defined share in the house. This would normally be half each, although you could have different fractions. You will then be able to gift or bequeath your share independently. This could have the advantage of utilising the £150,000 nil rate inheritance tax band which otherwise might not have been used.

9.4 Arranging Your Mortgage

You will probably need a mortgage to purchase the house. In any event, it may be advantageous to take a mortgage in order to benefit from tax relief on the interest. At present, this extends to the first £30,000 of your loan, spouses being considered as one for this purpose.

However, mortgage interest relief is much less beneficial than before. *See 2.12* Originally given at your full tax rate, it was then restricted to basic rate (25%). For 1994–5 the relief rate is 20%, with 15% applying for 1995–6.

In general, the relief is given under the MIRAS system. That stands for *See 2.13* Mortgage Interest Relief At Source. Under the MIRAS scheme you deduct tax at the appropriate rate (15% for 1995–6) on paying the interest.

You can borrow the money entirely yourself. Alternatively, the mortgage can be taken jointly by your spouse and yourself. This can have its tax advantages as is discussed below in connection with the separate taxation of spouses' income.

The mortgage will, of course, be secured on the house. However, the building society or bank who are lending you the money will also require a reliable way of being repaid the capital. The simplest is what is known as the repayments method.

You pay back part of the capital with each instalment. Thus, normally every month, you will pay interest and some capital. Only the interest element attracts tax relief and this eventually will reduce as the outstanding loan reduces.

Another method is to link your mortgage to a *life assurance endowment policy*. Instead of repaying the capital amount borrowed, you pay the premiums on the endowment policy, which has a capital sum assured, equal to the mortgage. You arrange for the mortgage and the policy to be of equal length and when the latter matures, you use the proceeds to pay off the former.

The life policy can be with or without profits. The latter is cheaper but the former is likely to prove the better investment. A 'low cost endowment policy' can also be used, which has a sum assured which is initially less than the loan. However, the prospective bonuses are taken into account. In the early years, some temporary life assurance often is included to cover the shortfall.

One advantage of the endowment method is that life cover is provided. Otherwise you (and perhaps your spouse) will need to arrange this separately. (Usually the lenders will require life cover.) Another point is that the amount of interest will fluctuate with rate changes but not reduce on account of the loan reducing. Thus, unless further withdrawn by the Government, the future flow of tax relief should continue.

But the endowment method is not nearly as beneficial from a tax point of view as it used to be. At one time, the life assurance premiums themselves attracted some tax relief. (This now only applies for pre-14 March 1984 policies.) Furthermore, as mentioned, the actual tax saved through interest relief has much diminished.

9.5   Linking Your Mortgage to Pensions or PEPs

If you wish to create an investment to repay your mortgage, why not use the most tax efficient? That is the argument behind linking your mortgage with a pension scheme or a Personal Equity Plan (PEP). However, in either case, you will need to make sure that your mortgage lenders will agree to such an arrangement.

What happens when you link your mortgage with a pension scheme is that you plan that your lump sum entitlement will be sufficient to repay the amount outstanding on the mortgage. You then commute the appropriate part of your pension and receive a tax-free lump sum out of which you pay off the mortgage at the required time. (Fuller details regarding commuting your pension are given in Chapter 12.)

See 12.2

This method does have the drawback of reducing the ongoing amount of your pension. However, it certainly maximises tax relief and makes good sense if you would otherwise not be making the maximum allowable contributions.

In general, personal pension plans are the best vehicles to use, since they are flexible and self-contained. However, if you belong to an occupational pension scheme, the lenders might agree that your mortgage is repaid out of your projected lump sum on retirement.

PEPs also provide a tax-efficient means of providing a fund to repay your mortgage. However, unlike pension arrangements, there is no tax relief when you invest the money.

Also see 9.13.4

The main tax advantages are that, in general, no tax is payable on the income of your PEP unless it is withdrawn. Also, no capital gains tax is payable. When your mortgage becomes repayable, you simply realise your PEP and this attracts no tax. Fuller details about PEPs are given elsewhere.

If your mortgage lenders agree to allowing your eventual repayment to be made out of a PEP, they will normally require you to put more money into your investment each year. For example, monthly instalments might be required. Generally, allowance would be made for a growth factor in calculating how much you should invest.

9.6 Profiting From Separate Taxation

Also see 10.6

It was only from 6 April 1990 that the 'fiscal knot' was broken. Previously, husband and wife were taxed as one, subject to an election regarding earned income only. After 5 April 1990, the income of each spouse is separately taxed. This means that a complete set of allowances and tax rate scales is available for each.

See 2.6–8

But it does not end there. There is the married couple's allowance, which goes to the husband unless his income is insufficient to use it. However, a joint election can be made to split it equally, or for the wife to take it entirely. What is more, you can still gift or sell assets to your spouse free of both capital gains tax and capital transfer tax.

There are other useful rules. For example, you and your spouse can elect how you wish to split the tax relief on your joint mortgage. Also, regarding a jointly held asset, you are automatically treated as having half of the income each. However, this is subject to the right to have the income divided for tax purposes in proportion to the shares in which you each own the asset.

All of these advantages are open to you when you are married. The important thing is that you plan to obtain the maximum benefit from them. The kind of benefits available are indicated in the following example.

9.7 Example: Separate Taxation

John Rich marries June Poor and for 1994–5 she has no income or capital gains. His substantial income and gains are shown below, as is his tax liability.

Salaries		£50,000
Freelance earnings		60,000
Dividends including tax credits		70,000
		180,000
Less personal relief	3,445	
pensions contributions	9,555	
		13,000
		£167,000
Income tax – £3,000 at 20%	600	
20,700 at 25%	5,775	
143,300 at 40%	57,320	
		63,695

Less married couple's allowance		
£1,720 at 20%	344	
Tax credits £70,000 at 20%	14,000	14,344
Net further income tax payable		£49,351
Capital gains for 1994–5	£15,000	
less annual exemption	5,800	
	£9,200	
Capital gains tax at 40%	£3,680	

Thus, John's tax bill will be a hefty £53,031 (£49,351 + £3,680). However, much tax can be saved if June has some of the income and gains. For example, suppose she owns some of the shares, so that her gross dividend income is £27,145 and makes £6,000 of the capital gains. The combined tax payable by the couple will be much less, as is seen below.

	John	June
Salaries and freelance	£110,000	–
Dividends (gross)	42,855	27,145
	152,855	27,145
Less personal relief	(3,445)	(3,445)
pensions contributions	(9,555)	–
	£139,855	£23,700
Income tax at 20%	600	600
25%	5,775	5,775
40% on 116,155	46,462	–
	52,837	6,375
Less married couple's allowance £1,720 × 20%	(344)	–

Tax credits on dividends

20% on £42,855	(8,571)	on £6,445	(1,289)
25% on £20,700			(5,775)
Income tax payable/repayable	43,922		£(689)
TOTAL		£43,233	

Capital gains	£9,000		£6,000
Less annual exemptions	5,800		5,800
	3,200		£200
Capital gains tax 40%	£1,280		25% £50
Total		£1,330	
Total tax (£43,233 + £1,330)		£44,563	

Thus, the couple's 1994–5 tax is down by £8,468 (£53,031–£44,563) through Jill having some of the income and gains.

9.8 How to Split Income and Gains

We have seen from the preceding example the tax savings to be made through splitting income and gains between husband and wife. The big question is how can this be done? Fortunately, the tax rules make this easier for married couples.

As we have seen, transfers of investments and other assets between spouses are normally free from capital gains tax (unless separated) and inheritance tax. This is a big help, since many of the following simple ways of splitting income and gains involve asset transfers.

See 9.9 ● If one spouse is in business, he or she can employ the other. A reasonable salary should be paid, depending upon the work involved. This is discussed in more detail below.

● Where one spouse has a family company, the other could be employed as perhaps company secretary or be a director. Again the pay should be reasonable or the Revenue may challenge it.

● Should both husband and wife be involved in a business (or profession) they could do so as a partnership. This is a good way to share the income, as is described below.

● Investments can be gifted from one spouse to the other. This transfers the income and also any capital gains on future sale. However, husband and wife will need to trust each other and newly weds in particular may not be that sure of each other.

When you are considering making fresh investments, do so in the name of your spouse. If an actual share purchase is involved, give your spouse the money, so that he or she can buy the shares.

● Investments such as shares, bank deposits and building society accounts can be put into joint names. This makes it safer for the donor, particularly if both spouses must sign. Also, you can elect to split the income between you in the proportions in which you own the asset, instead of being taxed on half each.

Thus, suppose John has a bank deposit account of £50,000. He can change this to a joint account in which June has a one-tenth share. In this case it would not be beneficial making the election, so that June is taxed on one half of the income although owning only one tenth. Thus the more heavily taxed John is divested of half the income through transferring only one tenth of the asset to June.

● Family company shares provide a particularly useful way of passing more income to your spouse. First transfer shares and then declare a substantial dividend, some of which will boost your spouse's income.

This may mean that you need to reduce your remuneration, but this will have the effect of cutting down on the National Insurance contributions payable. However, do not pay your spouse so much dividend as to put him or her into the higher rate band. Otherwise, the tax credit becomes worth only 20% instead of 25%.

● Where your spouse has family company shares, you can pass him or her more of the income by means of dividend waivers. This involves effecting a waiver before a dividend is declared and this causes no inheritance tax. The company can then declare a higher dividend per share, since you will receive none on your own shares. Of course, if other shareholders are involved, this method is less useful.

- There is another way of adjusting your respective taxable incomes which does not involve transferring any assets. This is to have a joint mortgage on your home and elect as to the proportions in which the interest is split for tax purposes. However, with the reduction in the value of the relief for the interest, this election has become less valuable. For 1994–5 the relief is 20% and for 1995–6 only 15%.

1995–6
£6,000

- Passing *capital gains* to your spouse is mainly a matter of transferring assets which are 'pregnant with gain'. The spouse later sells, making a taxable capital gains, and is able to benefit from any unused annual exemption (£5,800) and lower rate bands.

- New issues present a good opportunity for your spouse to make some capital gains. You can provide the funds and, subject to the investments performing well, they can be sold quickly at a good profit. In turn, this provides your spouse with capital gains which are free of tax up to the annual exemption of £5,800, unless already used.

Note that the income splitting election for jointly owned assets does not apply for capital gains. Thus, if you own 60% of an investment and your spouse 40%, you will be taxed on those respective percentages of any gain on sale. However, if the ownership split is not clear cut, the Inland Revenue will normally accept 50:50.

9.9 Employing Your Spouse

As mentioned above, one way of passing income to your spouse is by employing him or her. This can be done whether you are a sole trader or operate through one or more companies. Either way, your spouse can be made an employee and paid a salary. On the assumption that your income is substantially more than that of your spouse, this should result in good tax savings.

If you are a sole proprietor, your taxable profits will be reduced. Furthermore, as a company director, you will probably be able to take less salary on account of your spouse's pay. This, in turn, will reduce your tax bill.

Your spouse will pay less tax on her salary than you would have paid on the same amount, taken as the top slice of your income. This is because *See 2.6–8* you will have used up your personal allowance, lower rate band and often basic rate income tax band. However, your spouse will have at least some of the reliefs intact.

A further advantage of your spouse having earned income is that pension *See 8.2* contributions can be paid in his or her own right. If a company is the employer, either a personal pension scheme or an occupational pension scheme might be suitable. However, if you are self-employed, a personal pension scheme is the most likely.

Any pension scheme for your spouse will not restrict your own contributions. Thus, the cover for your spouse provides a valuable bonus, both in terms of extra tax relief and security at retirement.

You should take care that your spouse does sufficient work to justify the salary that he or she is being paid. The Inland Revenue could enquire as to this and disallow any excess. Accounting, secretarial and reception duties are suitable. So far as a company is concerned, the position of company secretary is appropriate and, if acceptable, that of director.

Be careful that the extra National Insurance contributions do not outweigh *1995–6* the tax savings. These arise under Class 1, as shown in the Appendix, and *£58* start at a salary level of £57 per week for 1994–5. Thus, provided you pay *See* your spouse no more than £56.99, no National Insurance is payable. *Appendix 16*

Thus, to avoid any contributions, the salary needs to be pegged to about *1995–6* £2,963. Above that, if your spouse had used none of his or her £3,445 *£3,525* personal allowance, by taking the salary up to that level will save an extra £85 or so net. This assumes your own tax rate is 40% and your earnings are correspondingly reduced.

Once your spouse's personal relief has been used up, there is the £3,000 *1995–6* lower rate band at 20%. This means that transferring from your 40% band *£3,200*

157

saves 20% income tax. However, the National Insurance payable could take a good chunk of this, since your spouse's contributions will be at 10%.

Other factors also need considering. Employer's National Insurance contributions will be payable in respect of your spouse. However, the employers will obtain tax relief on these.

At the same time, on the basis that your own salary is reduced, the employer's contributions on it will also fall. Similarly, if your salary falls sufficiently, your own contributions will go down. (There is a different position if you are self-employed and pay Class 4 contributions.) The interplay of these various factors is shown by the following example.

9.10 Example: Salary For Spouse

Tom is a director of a family company and his wife Jill is made an employee. Tom's salary is £40,000 and it is proposed to reduce this to £30,000, so as to pay Jill £10,000. Assuming that Jill has no other income and that the company pays the 25% small companies corporation tax rate, the net saving will be:

Tom saves income tax of £10,000 at 40%		£4,000
His own National Insurance contributions remain as before but those of the company are reduced by 10.2% of £10,000	£1,020	
Less tax relief at 25%	255	765
		4,765
Jill pays income tax on	£10,000	
Less personal relief	3,445	
	£6,555	
Tax payable £3,000 at 20%		600
£3,555 at 25%		889

158

National Insurance contributions:

Employee £2,963 at 2%		59		
£7,037 at 10%		704		
Employer £2,964	NIL			
£2,236 at 3.6%	80.50			
£2,340 at 5.6%	131.04			
£2,460 at 7.6%	186.96			
	398.50			
Less corporation tax relief 25%	99.62	299	2,551	
Net saving			£2,214	

Note This example is based on the income tax and National Insurance contribution rates for 1994–5. The net saving of £2,214 takes account of the tax and National Insurance of Tom, Jill and the company.

9.11 Husband and Wife Partnerships

See 2.20

If you are a sole trader, instead of employing your spouse, consider taking him or her into partnership. This can have various advantages, compared to an employment arrangement.

Provided a proper partnership deed is drawn up, it is unlikely that the Inland Revenue will dispute the amount of your spouse's share of the taxable profits. Your spouse should be shown as having, say, a half share or one-third and this will effectively split your earnings between the two of you.

Another advantage is that the extra cost of National Insurance contributions is much less than if you employ your spouse. In fact, there could even be a reduction in the combined amount. This is because you will both be paying Class 4 contributions, which apply at 7.3% on the earnings band from £6,490 to £22,360.

See App. 16

1995–6 £6,640– £22,880

For example, suppose your earnings as a sole trader are £26,000. You will pay Class 4 contributions at the maximum level, which is £1,158.51 for 1994–5. However, if your spouse is a 50% partner, there is a saving.

As equal partners you will each have earnings of £13,000. So you each pay Class 4 contributions at 7.3% on £13,000–£6,490 making £475.23. Thus between you, only £950.46 is payable, a reduction of £208.05.

Income tax savings result from husband and wife partnerships which are similar to those described where you employ your spouse. Thus, in the example given, if neither you nor your spouse has any other income, as a sole trader your top tax rate on £26,000 less personal and married couple's relief is 25%.

By making your spouse an equal partner, you will be reducing your income tax bill by £13,000 at 25%. At the same time, £13,000 will be taxed in the hands of your spouse. £3,445 will be covered by personal relief and £3,000 taxed at 20%. This leaves £2,555 at 25%, on which no saving results. Thus the income tax saved for 1994–5 is:

Income	Old tax rate	New tax rate	Tax saving	
£3,445	25%	nil	25%	£861.25
£3,000	25%	20%	5%	£150.00
£2,555	25%	25%	nil	–
Total income tax saving				£1,011.25

Much larger tax savings may arise from husband and wife partnerships if these result in any earnings being removed from 40% tax. Thus, suppose your earnings as a sole trader are £60,000 and your spouse becomes an equal partner. If he or she has no other income, the income tax saved will be:

£3,445 at 40%	£1,378
£3,000 at 20 (40–20)%	£600
£20,700 at 15 (40–25)%	£3,105
Total income tax saving	£5,083

As mentioned, provided there is a proper partnership agreement and your spouse takes part in running the business, the Inland Revenue are unlikely to object to the size of his or her profit share. However, there are professional requirements to consider in some cases.

Suppose that you are in professional practice as, say, an accountant or solicitor. Your professional body may only allow your spouse to join you in practice if he or she also belongs to that organisation.

9.12   Drawing Up Your Wills

Also see 10.14

You have only recently got married. So why worry about wills at this stage? The answer depends partly on how wealthy you are and partly on whether you would both be happy with the effect of the intestacy rules. Those rules cover the distribution of the assets of a person who dies without leaving a will.

The first point to note is that if you have a will already, it will probably be revoked automatically when you marry. An exception is where your will contemplates your actual marriage and you intend that it remains valid afterwards.

If you do not make a will and leave children, your spouse takes the first £125,000 on your death and your children take a life interest in half the residue, the rest going to your wife.

But if you have no children, your spouse takes the first £200,000 and half of the remainder. Your parents take the rest of your estate or, if they are dead, your brothers and sisters inherit this. Only if you have no children, parents, brothers or sisters who survive you can you be sure that your spouse will obtain all of your assets under the intestacy rules.

Thus, making a will soon after you marry is likely to have the main object of ensuring the destination of your assets, should you die. Inheritance tax savings at this stage are secondary. For example, if you want your spouse to inherit all of your assets, you should make a will to this effect. He or she is likely to do exactly the same.

When one of you dies, no inheritance tax will be payable since everything

See 3.25
1995–6
£154,000 is going to the surviving spouse. However, the benefit of using the £150,000 nil rate band is lost, although the survivor could execute a deed of variation as described in Chapter 12. This might be used to redirect *See 12.16* sufficient funds to others, to cover the nil rate band.

On the other hand, you may wish that certain of your assets do not pass to your surviving spouse. For example you may have a large shareholding in your family company but your spouse takes no interest in this.

However, your brother may work with you in the business and so you might wish to leave him the shares. As to the possible inheritance tax *See 3.32.5* payable, the value of the shares may be covered by the nil rate band. Also, 100% or 50% business property relief is likely to be available.

See 10.4, 11.16 & 12.15 As you will see in later chapters, you should constantly review your will, as should your spouse. Changes are appropriate at various stages in your life. Examples are when a child is born or when your fortunes change. Sometimes, it will suffice to append a codicil. This simply adds to or varies your existing will.

9.13 Tax-Efficient Investment

Being newly married, it is quite likely that you will have no spare funds to invest. However, if you are in a good job, or prospering in your own business, you may have available money for investment. The following tax-efficient investments should be considered.

9.13.1

National Savings Bank ordinary deposits are a useful investment for limited funds which you may need at short notice. The first £70 of interest each year is free of tax.

9.13.2

Index-linked Savings Bonds should only be bought if you can envisage being able to hold them for the stipulated time necessary to obtain full benefits. They then attract indexing and a percentage bonus, both of which are tax free.

9.13.3

Pension schemes of various kinds have been considered previously. Whether your employer provides the scheme or you contribute to your own personal pension plans, the tax advantages are huge.

See 8.2 etc.

9.13.4

Personal Equity Plans (PEPs) enable you to invest directly or indirectly in equities. Subject to the rules, the dividends are tax free, as are the capital gains. However, the expenses charged by the managers must be considered and make PEPs of no value to non-taxpayers.

See also 4.10

Every year, you and your spouse are each allowed to invest £9,000 in PEPs. This includes £3,000 in single company PEPs. You can cash in PEPs whenever you wish.

9.13.5

Tax Efficient Special Savings Accounts (TESSAs) are a safer form of investment than PEPs. You and your spouse are allowed one each and effectively you have a building society or bank deposit account on which the interest is tax free.

See also 4.10

The arrangements lasts for five years and no capital should be withdrawn during that time. Otherwise, all tax savings are lost. Income can be withdrawn subject to a 25% tax deduction.

There are maximum investment levels. The total cannot be more than £9,000, with yearly limits of £3,000 in the first year and £1,800 in each of the others. Thus, if the annual limits are reached, only £600 can be invested in the final year.

9.13.6

If you have a large income, then you might consider investing in *Enterprise Investment Schemes* (EIS) shares. You can invest up to £100,000 each year, as can your spouse. You obtain tax relief on your investment at 20%, which is set against your general income tax bill.

See also 4.8

Note that the relief is lost if you dispose of your EIS shares within five years. Subject to this, there is no capital gains tax when you sell the shares. EIS shares are often risky investments and you must be selective. However, they carry valuable tax savings.

9.14   Planning List – Newly Married

● Parents and grandparents in particular should make good use of the inheritance tax marriage gifts exemptions.

● Purchase your home jointly and, for tax planning purposes, as tenants in common.

● Raise the finance you require to buy your home in a tax-efficient manner. Take a mortgage secured to an endowment policy, a pension or PEP.

● Aim to maximise the benefits of separate taxation by splitting income and gains with your spouse through:

employing your spouse
partnership with your spouse
gifting investments
putting investments into joint names
gifting family company shares and paying dividends
providing funds for investment such as in new issues.

● Where you have a joint investment or mortgage, consider making the appropriate splitting election.

● Consider making wills.

● Seek tax-efficient forms of investment such as:

National Savings Bank ordinary deposits and index-linked bonds
PEPs
TESSAs
EIS investments
Pension schemes.

CHAPTER TEN

Parenthood

10.1

'Familiarity breeds contempt – and children.' So wrote Mark Twain with a certain wry cynicism. However, the arrival of your first child certainly marks the start of a new stage in your life for tax-planning purposes.

The patter of little feet signals important new tax-saving opportunities. These may involve three or even four generations. As well as your spouse and yourself, grandparents and any living great-grandparents may wish to make tax-saving arrangements to benefit the children.

Of course, the older members of the family may take a little persuading that the arrival of a new baby should be marked in this way. In fact, it may be that the family solicitor or accountant is better placed to give this advice than you are.

This is the time when you are likely to have a growing income but also the highest expenditure. Thus, help in meeting the costs of bringing up the children is most opportune. This might be provided in a durable and tax-efficient way, by means of a discretionary settlement or accumulation and maintenance trust set up by a grandparent.

When you enter the parenthood stage, the new arrival(s) may well take up a large part of your attention. However, other important developments are likely to occur which will create openings for tax savings. Matters covered by this chapter include:

10.2   The Scope For Children to Have Income and Capital Gains

See 6.7   This matter has already been considered in Chapter 6. As was pointed out, a new-born baby is entitled to an array of tax allowances. Tax savings are thus possible through arranging for infants to have income and capital gains. This often involves gifting assets to them and making settlements.

10.2.1

As previously discussed, the *capital gains tax* consequences of gifts and settlements for the giver must be watched. Capital gains tax is payable on the gift of an asset, as if it were sold at market value. However, in the case of certain classes of gift, elections can be made to hold over any gains.

The main instances are family trading company shares, business assets used in your trade, etc. and agricultural property. The election can also be made regarding gifts which give rise to inheritance tax immediately (even if of NIL amount), such as to discretionary settlements.

1995–6
£6,000
£3,200
£21,100

The big advantage is that the child has the full annual capital gains tax exemption of £5,800. Also bands of £3,000 taxed at 20% and £20,700 at 25% are available, to the extent not applied to income. Thus, gains arising on asset sales by the child (including held-over gains) may well carry little or no tax.

10.2.2

Inheritance tax is far less likely to arise on gifts (provided the giver survives for at least seven years). However, an exception is where a discretionary trust is created or augmented. This would result in tax at half of the full rate (20%) after allowing for the normal reliefs and unused nil rate band.

Also see 6.9–12

The most important reliefs to be considered are those for business property and for agricultural property. Reference to previous chapters indicates that the relief is at either 100% or 50%. The 100% relief applies to gifts out of holdings above 25% in unquoted trading companies, below which the 50% rate applies.

See 3.32.5

Thus, suppose you settle part of your 20% holding of shares in the family trading company, on discretionary trusts. The 50% business property relief is available. As a result, if the value of the settled shares is no more than £312,000, there is no inheritance tax. This is on the basis that your £150,000 nil rate band is intact and you have used none of your £3,000 annual exemption for this or last year.

1995–6 £320,000 £154,000

Investments can be put into the name of a child and, unless these come from the parents, any tax deducted from the income can be reclaimed. If the investments do come from the parents, they are taxed on the income, unless the aggregate amount for the tax year is no more than £100.

Thus, suppose your father gives your ten-year-old son John 10,000 £1 shares in the family company and a dividend of 80% is paid during 1994–5. This amounts to £8,000 with a £2,000 tax credit. Assuming John has no other income, his tax position is:

Dividend and tax credit	£10,000
Personal relief	£3,445
	£6,555

Income tax

£3,000 at 20%	600.00
£3,555 at 25% reduced to 20%	711.00
	1,311.00
Tax credit	2,000.00
Income tax repayable	£689.00

This position is much better than if you had given John the shares. In that case, you will be taxed on the income. This results in no extra tax, if you pay no more than the basic rate (25%). However, if you are a higher rate payer, you have an extra liability as follows:

Tax at 40% on £10,000	£4,000
Tax credit	£2,000
Further income tax payable	£2,000

So, instead of £689.00 being reclaimed, you pay £2,000. Thus there is a clear tax advantage to be gained if your father gives the shares to John.

If you wish to gift investments to your children without risking being taxed on the income, choose those with no income that is taxable. Good examples are National Savings Certificates and Index Linked Bonds. These are tax free and so you will have no tax liability if you gift them to your child.

If you give your child life assurance single premium bonds, these are free of basic rate tax, although there may be some higher rate liability on encashment. This can normally be avoided if encashment is deferred until the child reaches age 18 (or marries earlier).

10.3   Trusts Established by Grandparents

Parenthood involves substantially increased expenditure, so any help with the cost is welcome, particularly if this is supplemented by the taxman. As seen above, gifts and settlements from grandparents are likely to be more tax efficient than those you might make as a parent.

Regarding trusts, these may already exist, with your child included in the class of beneficiaries. An example would be where your father created a discretionary settlement whose beneficiaries include yourself, your wife and any future issue. As and when any children are born, they will automatically become beneficiaries.

Thus, the trustees of such an existing discretionary settlement would normally be able to distribute income for your child. This would carry with it a tax credit of $\frac{35}{65}$ths, all or part of which can be reclaimed.

For example, your five-year-old daughter Joy has no other income for 1994–5 and £6,500 is paid for her maintenance by your father's discretionary trust. Income tax is reclaimable as follows:

Income distribution	£6,500
Tax credit $\frac{35}{65}$ths	3,500
	10,000
Personal allowance	3,445
	£6,555
Income tax £3,000 at 20%	600.00
£3,555 at 25%	888.75
	1,488.75
Tax credit	3,500.00
Income tax repayable	£2,011.25

See 6.14 If none of the grandparents have existing settlements, they may be prepared to set up one or more of them. Since we are considering your children, accumulation and maintenance settlements are best and these are examined in Chapter 6.

However, discretionary settlements are also an option, especially if there are abundant funds. These have the advantage of greater flexibility regarding the ultimate destination of the income and capital.

A wider class of beneficiaries can be included, with the trustees having discretion as to who benefits. (In tax-effective accumulation and maintenance settlements, no beneficiary can have reached age 25 at the outset.) Thus, discretionary settlements may appeal to the grandparents as vehicles for looking after all of their family.

See 7.5 But the inheritance tax drawbacks of discretionary settlements cannot be overlooked. As outlined in Chapter 7, inheritance tax is payable at 20% on amounts settled, once the exemptions and nil rate band are exceeded. Also, there are exit and ten-year charges to contend with.

Furthermore, there is much to be said for the selectivity of accumulation and maintenance trusts. Normally your children alone would be covered and their entitlements would be clearly defined.

As previously indicated, the children would need to obtain an interest in possession (a share of income as of right) from an age not exceeding 25. Prior to that, the income could be accumulated or used for the maintenance and education of the children. Often, from age 18, income is paid direct to them.

The position regarding the capital is that the trust deed will direct an age (say 35) at which each beneficiary obtains a share. However, discretion is sometimes given to the trustees to defer such distribution. They might do this if they consider that the beneficiary is not yet sufficiently mature to receive the capital.

Remember that if all four grandparents have the necessary funds and wish to do so, they can each establish trusts. This spreads the risk of any inheritance tax arising, such as on setting up accumulation and maintenance trusts. Furthermore, it increases the scope for small discretionary settlements within the £150,000 nil rate band.

1995–6
£154,000

It is also worth considering whether grandparents should alter their wills so as to include one or more trusts. These could include their grand-children. After that, the will may need updating from time to time to keep up with changes.

The subject of deeds of variation is dealt with in later chapters. However, note that they can be used to create a trust through the will of a person who died within the last two years. This might be done out of the £150,000 nil rate inheritance tax band which otherwise would not have been used, such as where the original will left all the estate to the surviving spouse.

See 11.16.2 & 12.16

For example, suppose your father dies and leaves all of his estate to your mother, no inheritance tax being payable. You are an only child and have two young children.

Your mother has ample other funds for her future security and so she agrees to a deed of variation putting £150,000 of the estate into a settlement for the benefit of your children. This is treated as having been done at the date of your father's death and results in no inheritance tax or capital gains tax.

1995–6
£154,000

An accumulation and maintenance settlement could be used in this exer-cise. However, if your mother is not sure that she will have enough funds for the future, a discretionary settlement might be created through the deed of variation. Your mother could then be included as a beneficiary in case of need.

The main benefits of creating settlements in this way for the benefit of your children are twofold. Funds are taken out of the estate of the surviving grandparent, so that substantial inheritance tax is saved. At the same time, your children obtain income and ultimately capital in a tax-efficient way.

171

10.4   Parental Settlements

No matter how dearly your parents and parents-in-law love your children, they may not wish to settle money on them. Be that as it may, you and your spouse can do so, if you have the means.

It is true that if you settle money on your infant children, the tax disadvantages mentioned above will be in point. However, with careful planning, the disadvantages of your being taxed on trust income distributions to the children can be minimised.

You could set up an accumulation and maintenance settlement which makes no income distributions to your children until they reach their eighteenth birthdays. It is true that the income will be taxed at 35% in the trust, but this is better than your own tax rate if you are in the 40% bracket.

No matter what sort of trusts are involved, the problem is minimised if assets are owned which produce little or no income. For example, a house occupied by the family might be settled. Also, holdings of family company shares come into this category, if no dividends are paid.

A further possibility is that either you or your spouse has a small income, so that allowances and tax rate bands are not fully used. This may well be the case if, say, the wife stays at home looking after the young children.

It would then make sense for her to create an accumulation and maintenance settlement whose income is used for the children. She will be taxed on that income. However, the tax will be mitigated because of her unused allowances and 20/25% bands.

If you can afford it, settling money on your children makes good sense from an inheritance tax point of view. This is so, even if you have just entered the parenthood stage. You are reducing your estate, so that any future inheritance tax liability is cut.

Furthermore, by acting at an early stage, you are reducing the risk of there being radical changes in the political system. However, you should try to ensure that the settlement deeds guard against the children obtaining funds prematurely.

10.5 School Fee Planning

Parenthood brings with it the desire and/or need to plan for each child's future. The most obvious direction for this is regarding education. If you are thinking of fee-paying schools, it makes good sense to provide for the cost in a tax-efficient way.

There was a time when sophisticated arrangements were of considerable value in school fee planning. For example, there were scholarship schemes producing valuable tax savings. Also, deeds of covenant from grandparents and others were much used.

However, the tax advantages have been legislated against over the years. The result is that planning is more likely to be of a general variety, along the lines of the suggestions put forward in Chapter 6. These include trusts, savings through PEPs, qualifying life assurance policies and single *See 6.17* premium bonds.

A very good way of meeting the cost of school fees is from the income of trusts. However, if you as a parent are the settlor of the trust, you will be taxed on any income applied in this way, since it is regarded as your child's and hence yours for tax purposes. This has been explained earlier.

Trusts set up by grandparents are ideal vehicles for paying school fees, since the appropriate income is treated as the children's for tax purposes. *See 10.3* As described earlier, this frequently results in tax repayments for them. In turn, this increases the money available for the education and maintenance of the children.

Both discretionary and accumulation and maintenance settlements are useful for paying school fees. If your parents or parents-in-law have spare funds and are sufficiently generous, they might well consider both types. The former offer more flexibility, whilst the latter are more specifically directed to the children concerned.

Also, as previously indicated, if larger discretionary settlements are used, immediate inheritance tax liabilities may arise. However, where a *See 7.5* grandparent has made no chargeable transfers in the previous seven *1995–6* years, normally at least £156,000 can be settled without any immediate *£160,000* inheritance tax. (This takes account of the £150,000 nil rate band and two years' annual exemption.)

But what if settlements by grandparents are out of the question? Then it is up to you as parents. In that case, the answer would rarely be a trust. It is rather more a matter of building up suitable investments to use when the time comes for paying the fees.

Another point is that you may not be sure as to whether your children's education will be done privately at all. When your first child is born, you will not know how many others will follow and may find that you cannot educate them all privately. In that case, you may decide that the fairest thing is to deal with them all alike and send them to state schools.

Furthermore, there may be a good state school in your area, so that you prefer to send your children there. Of course, much will depend upon your own and your spouse's income and prospects. If these are good, you can put aside funds for education with increased confidence.

To obtain the most benefit, you should start investing as soon as possible. If you are using PEPs, you and your spouse can each put £6,000 into a general PEP and £3,000 into a single company PEP. Charges are payable, but the income and capital gains are tax free.

Up to the amounts mentioned, you can put in what you can afford each year and, when school fees are payable, cash in what you need. Be careful how you select the funds in which to invest. Subject to this, your investments should grow, providing a source from which to pay the fees. Any PEPs not used in this way will remain as a worthwhile investment.

Using qualifying life assurance policies to fund school fees is a less flexible method. Such a policy normally involves premiums for at least ten years. At the end of its term, you will receive a tax-free sum which could be used to pay school fees.

Non-qualifying life assurance policies are less attractive for tax purposes, but are more flexible. For example, you could invest in a single premium bond and, when necessary, withdraw up to 5% each year. These withdrawals are not taxed until the policy is surrendered, etc. Then you will be charged on any profits broadly at the difference between your top tax rate and the basic rate.

10.6   Separate Taxation

In Chapter 9 the question of maximising the benefits of separate taxation was covered, particularly as relating to the newly married. However, the position may well change as the parenthood stage is entered. *See 9.6*

In particular, one spouse may choose to devote his or her time to looking after the children, at least for some years. Both spouses may share the load, but if one of them is going to stop working to concentrate on the children, this is likely to be the wife.

The effect for previously working wives will be that their incomes will plummet. Even if they have investment income, it may still not be enough to cover their personal reliefs and lower tax bands. Hence there is much scope for tax saving through redistributing assets and income.

Full details of 'how to split income and gains' are given in Chapter 9. Do not overlook the election options regarding joint mortgages and invest- ment holdings. These are a good way to boost the wife's income on a temporary basis. *See 9.8*

Another way in which the wife can have a temporary income boost is where she owns family company shares, as does her husband. He can then waive the dividends on his own shares, so that more funds are available to be paid to her.

If the wife is at home looking after the children, she may still be able to work in her husband's business or profession on a part-time basis. As discussed in Chapter 9, this is a useful way for her to supplement her income, but the National Insurance position should be watched. *See 9.9*

10.7   Tax Planning Related to Your Business or Professional Advancement

The parenthood phase considered by this chapter is a long one. It would normally start in your twenties or thirties and continue for 20 years or more. During this time, not only will your children be growing up, but your business or professional activities are likely to develop. As a result, you should not only concentrate your tax-planning activities on your children, but also, your own affairs will need careful attention.

Reference to Chapter 8 on 'Early Working Life' will give many pointers to the avenues that tax planning can take regarding business and employment. The same ideas that were then considered for Tom, the employee, Dick in the family business and Harry, the entrepreneur, hold good at this older stage in their lives. Therefore only some of the items are discussed below.

Particular subjects considered in subsequent sections are pensions, incorporation and working overseas. However, many other tax-efficient 'perks' are available. In view of your position hopefully improving, at least some of these may be suitable for you.

For example, it will make increasing sense for Tom to become a member of any share option schemes operated by his employers as he moves up in his company. This makes commercial sense for the employers too, since such schemes provide a real incentive for directors and employees.

10.7.1

Also see 8.4.4 Under an *approved share option scheme*, Tom will be able to buy large quantities of shares. The options at the time of grant can have a maximum value of £100,000 or four times his current earnings or those for the previous year. Since he can exercise his options once three years have elapsed from the time they were granted to him, there is then scope for obtaining more at that stage.

Subject to certain rules, Tom will only be charged to capital gains tax when he sells the shares which he acquired on exercising his options. This means that he will have the benefit of indexation relief on the price he paid and also any unused annual allowance.

For example, Tom is a higher rate tax payer and buys shares for £20,000 under his company's approved share option scheme. He sells the shares two years later in 1994–5 for £40,000, having used none of his annual allowance for that year. His capital gains tax is:

Proceeds		
Less: Cost	£20,000	
Indexation say 10%	2,000	22,000
		18,000
Less: Annual Allowance		5,800
		£12,200
Capital gains tax at 40%		£4,880

(If income tax would have applied to the gains, this would have been £20,000 at 40% = £8,000.)

To some extent, the nature of Tom's work will have a bearing on what particular 'perks' he has. For example, as previously discussed, the decision as to whether it is tax effective for a car to be provided partly depends on his business mileage. However, general company policy may result in his having a car at a certain stage.

10.8 Pensions

In Chapter 8, the great attractions of pension arrangements were examined both regarding tax and otherwise. As their incomes increase, Tom, Dick and Harry will all have scope for obtaining greater pensions cover.

See 8.2

Any pensions contributions made by his employers for Tom are likely to be geared to his salary. Furthermore, if the scheme is contributory, Tom's own contributions will increase with his salary. Thus, even though Tom may be finding the costs of raising a young family somewhat burdensome, his pension cover will be increasing automatically.

However, once his financial position improves, Tom would be well advised to supplement his basic scheme by paying extra contributions into an

AVC or FSAVC scheme. An additional voluntary contribution (AVC) scheme may be provided by his employers. Otherwise, Tom can use a free-standing additional voluntary contribution scheme (FSAVC).

Either way, Tom will be able to contribute up to 15% of his salary, provided the basic company scheme is non-contributory. Otherwise, his AVC or FSAVC contributions will be correspondingly reduced.

Thus, supposing Tom's salary is £40,000 and he contributes 5% to the company pension scheme. He will be able to make contributions to an AVC scheme provided by his employer as follows:

Total allowed contributions	15% of £40,000	£6,000
Less: contributions to company pension scheme	5% of £40,000	2,000
Maximum contributions to AVC scheme		£4,000

See 8.6.1 Dick, in the family business, probably has more flexible pension arrangements. There may be a self-administered scheme or executive pension arrangements for him. Furthermore, his pension is likely to be on a money purchase basis. That is to say that the fund will provide a lump sum to purchase his retirement benefits.

The maximum executive pension plan contributions payable each year go up as Dick gets older, subject to new rules operating from 1 September 1994. The limits for new schemes started subsequently are much lower than for earlier ones.

At age 30 the new limit for employee's plus employer's contributions is about 31% of salary instead of over 110%. However, for schemes existing at 1 September 1994, the new levels are being phased in over a five-year period.

Thus if Dick's company is having a successful year, he should consider maximising his pension contributions. This may even mean increasing

178

his salary in order to pay extra contributions both from the company and himself.

Harry, the entrepreneur, may have pension arrangements like Tom or Dick, but he may well prefer the independence of personal pension schemes. These provide excellent scope for directing the tax relief to the years when most needed.

Also see 8.12

Suppose that Harry discovers that for the previous tax year, his net relevant earnings were £100,000 and he is aged 40. For that year, 1993–4, he only paid £4,000 contributions to a personal pension scheme. He could have paid 20% of the £75,000 earnings cap, making £15,000, an extra £11,000.

However, Harry has until 5 April 1995 to pay all or part of the £11,000. If he so elects by 5 July 1995, these contributions (or part of them) can be carried back for tax relief purposes to 1993–4. Furthermore, Harry still will be able to make contributions in 1994–5, attracting relief for that year. Another valuable rule enables Harry to make extra contributions out of unused relief for the six previous years, as shown in the following example.

10.9 Example: Using Personal Pension Relief Carried Forward

Harry's available personal pension relief and contributions actually made for previous years have been as follows:

Tax Year	1988–9	1989–90	1990–1	1991–2	1992–3	1993–4
	(£)	(£)	(£)	(£)	(£)	(£)
Available relief	10,000	9,000	12,000	11,000	14,000	15,000
Contributions	6,000	7,000	7,000	9,000	9,000	10,000
Unused balances	4,000	2,000	5,000	2,000	5,000	5,000

Total unused relief	£23,000

Thus Harry will be able to make contributions in 1994–5 of up to £23,000 in excess of those allowed for that year. If less than the full amount is used, carried forward relief will be used up for the earlier years before the later ones.

10.10   Incorporation

See 8.13 When we met Harry in Chapter 8, he considered incorporating his business. However, the income tax savings needed to be weighed against the extra national insurance contributions.

But Harry is a shrewd businessman and as time has progressed, his affairs have prospered. He now has a substantial business and if he has not already incorporated, this should be a priority. This decision is partly related to tax and partly to commercial matters, such as the benefits of limited liability.

With a growing business, a particular advantage of incorporating is the ability to store up profits at a moderate tax rate. Instead of taking extra salary and dividends, Harry should leave profits in the company. Assuming that the profits are no more than £300,000 (and there are no associated companies) corporation tax at 25% will apply.

Thus, 75% of the profits will be retained in the company to build up the business and provide money for expansion. If Harry draws out extra director's remuneration, he will probably pay 40% income tax. At the same time, the company pays extra national insurance contributions.

If Harry takes dividends, he has a 20% tax credit to set against his 40% rate, which leaves 20%. At the same time the company pays 20% as advance corporation tax and the balance of its 25% rate later. Thus, arguably, 45% is payable in all.

So even if the full 33% corporation tax rate applies, it is tax efficient to retain profits in the company. However, Harry should be sure to draw sufficient for the needs of his family and make adequate pension contributions.

Capital gains tax may be payable on some of the assets which go into the company when Harry incorporates his business. In particular, goodwill may give rise to a large gain. However, relief is available if Harry puts the business into the company as a going concern, in exchange for shares. The gain is not taxed until he disposes of the shares.

The same rules apply for incorporating a partnership. In fact, if Harry has been trading in partnership with his wife, they may both be liable to capital gains tax if the company buys their shares for cash.

However, if the prospective capital gains are only modest, they may be covered by the couple's annual exemptions of £5,800 each. In those circumstances, it may be better not to take the consideration in shares. There will be no roll-over relief, but a higher base value for the shares will be obtained.

1995–6
£6,000

10.11 Working Abroad

In Chapter 8, the effect of Tom working overseas was considered and the same situation may well arise at this stage in his life. Of course, it will be more of an upheaval now that he has a wife and family. But if suitable relocation arrangements are made, Tom and his wife may well decide that the move will be worthwhile.

See 8.5

As previously explained, Tom should aim to be treated as neither resident nor ordinarily resident of the UK. This will normally exempt him from UK tax on his overseas income and worldwide capital gains.

See 2.21.2

Nevertheless, there are rules which fully exempt income from an overseas employment which Tom has during a 'qualifying period' of absence from the UK of at least one year. An overseas employment is one, the duties of which are performed outside this country.

Any UK duties which are purely incidental to the overseas employment are normally disregarded. Thus, if Tom works for an overseas subsidiary of a UK parent company, it would be in order for him to attend occasional meetings here.

A qualifying period does not need to be a tax year and certain visits to the UK are allowed. These are restricted to one-sixth of the qualifying period and 62 days is the maximum for any visit. The one-sixth test applies to all periods cumulatively from the start of Tom's qualifying period until the end of each overseas visit.

Dick and Harry may also spend periods working overseas. (By this time, Harry is operating through a UK group with overseas subsidiaries.) So far as employment (including directorships) is concerned, the same rules will apply as for Tom. However, they may also plan to work overseas more as a tax-saving device.

For example, if a large capital gain is in prospect, they might cease to be resident and ordinarily resident before it is realised (see Chapter 11). In *See 11.9* this way, capital gains tax is avoided, provided the rules are satisfied.

A more likely scenario for Dick and Harry is that they remain resident, ordinarily resident and domiciled in the UK. This means that subject to the 100% relief mentioned above, they will pay UK tax on their overseas salaries. (Double tax relief may be available regarding overseas tax.)

Presumably, they will be continuing to receive salaries from UK directorships, etc. In these circumstances, they may prefer to draw no money from the overseas companies and allow profits to accumulate abroad, possibly at a lower tax rate.

However, care must be taken about the Controlled Foreign Company (CFC) rules which apply to non-resident companies which are under overall UK control. This would particularly apply where Dick or Harry are directors of UK companies which have overseas subsidiaries, of which they are also directors.

If the overseas tax rate is less than 75% of what it would be in the UK, broadly 50% of the profits of trading companies (90% for investment companies) must be paid in dividends. Otherwise, any UK companies holding at least 10% of the overseas company's shares may be taxed on part of the profits under the CFC rules.

10.12 Tax-Efficient Investment

Having a young family, your expenses are likely to absorb at least a large part of your income. As discussed earlier, make sure that you have adequate pension cover. To the extent that you have any spare money, you should seek other profitable investment opportunities.

In particular, various types of investment are free of tax, or afford special *See 9.13* tax benefits as indicated in Chapter 9. These include TESSAs, PEPs and

EIS shares; also National Savings Certificates and Index-Linked Bonds.

VCTS *from 6.4.95*

The scope for using TESSAs is limited. Broadly, the most you can have invested is £9,000 plus accrued interest and your spouse can have the same. But the £9,000 you can each put into PEPs annually can grow into a considerable sum over the years, taking account of tax-free income.

As your tax rates increase, it will make sense for you to concentrate on investments producing capital gains, rather than income. It is true that the tax rates will be the same. However, capital gains are reduced by indexation relief, as well as the annual exemption, which is currently £5,800.

1995–6 £6,000

Thus, if you make direct investments into the stock market, concentrate on growth shares with low yields. Another, more risky way of creating capital gains is by using options to purchase or sell shares.

10.13   Capital Tax Planning

An aspect of capital gains tax has just been touched on. This is making full use of your £5,800 annual exemption each year. This mainly applies if you have a share portfolio. If 5 April approaches and you have not used your full allowance, consider using the 'bed and breakfast' technique.

1995–6 £6,000

What you do is to sell quoted shares one day and buy them back no earlier than the next. The sales crystallise gains which are set against your exemption. The repurchases stand on their own and result in your obtaining higher base values. (Naturally, if you do not wish to retain certain shareholdings, you do not buy them back.)

So far as inheritance tax is concerned, this has been discussed earlier in this chapter regarding trusts for your children. You can make gifts to them each year within your £3,000 annual exemption and these will not even be PETs. They will not count for inheritance tax at all.

See 10.3 etc.

However, if you are gifting investments, or your child invests your cash gift, you will be taxed on the income unless the aggregate for the tax year is no more than £100. Thus income-free investments make sense in these circumstances, as indicated earlier.

Also see
9.12 &
10.14

10.14   Changing Your Will

The birth of a child is a sensible time for your spouse and yourself to alter your wills (or make them if none exist). Even if your estates are modest and you wish to leave everything to your survivor and vice versa, assuming you wish to include your child on the second death, you should do so. As you become wealthier, you should aim at leaving at least the nil rate band (£150,000) to others than the surviving spouse. As pointed out, this will save £60,000 (£150,000 × 40%) under the present rules. If you wish this to go to the children, the money will need to be held in trust for them until at least age 18.

1995–6
£154,00

You may choose to include more sophisticated trusts in your will. For example, you could have an accumulation and maintenance settlement for your child or children. Another possibility is to have a discretionary trust created by your will. One advantage is that your spouse could be included in case of need.

See 6.14

See 7.5

Note that the will trusts only take effect when you die. Hopefully this will not happen for many years and so the provisions should be reviewed regularly and changed as necessary.

10.15   Planning List – Parenthood

●   Put income and gains into the children's hands to use their tax allowances.

●   Establish and use settlements to benefit the children, with grandparents or parents as settlors.

●   Provide for school fees in a tax-efficient way.

●   Maximise the benefits of separate taxation, allowing for the loss in the wife's earnings during pregnancy and after.

●   Plan for tax savings related to developments in your business or professional career, including:

pensions
incorporation
working overseas.

- Take advantage of opportunities for tax-efficient investments, such as PEPs, TESSAs and high gain/low income shares (more risky).

- Use your annual exemptions for capital gains tax (if necessary with 'bed and breakfasting') and for inheritance tax.

- Change your will when children are born.

CHAPTER ELEVEN

Middle Age

11.1

We have now reached the sixth stage, middle age, and this is the hardest to define. Certainly, Shakespeare's 'seven ages' has nothing equivalent; in fact his nearest is the fifth age:

> ... the Justice in fair round belly with good capon lined,
> With eyes severe and beard of formal cut,
> Full of wise saws and modern instances.

But you may look after your weight and not have a beard, so how are you to know you have reached this stage? You may, like me, think that middle age is something that is reached by your contemporaries but never yourself. However, you know that it applies to you when your children grow up, leave school and university, get married and have children of their own.

As you advance into middle age, your tax planning is more likely to involve giving than receiving. At all events, you should have more funds available. This is because your outgoings will probably reduce, especially when your children complete their education. One effect of this is that if you are so disposed, you may wish to make more charitable donations.

Many of the topics covered in previous chapters are equally important now, if not more so. One of the most vital points is that you may well be in a better financial position to take advantage of tax planning. Thus, you can now consider steps that you could not afford when you were younger.

So far as capital tax planning is concerned, you and your spouse are more likely to be the donors and settlors. However, this is by no means always so, since your respective parents and other relations may wish to benefit you.

Another important point is that, hopefully, your children are becoming better at handling their finances. Thus, you will be able to make gifts to them with increased confidence that they will deal with the funds responsibly.

Middle age often sees exciting business developments. You may sell out and/or buy new businesses. You may take early retirement and even settle abroad.

Topics dealt with in this chapter include:

11.2   Capital Gains Tax Relief on Buying and Selling Family Companies and Businesses

Also see 12.6

The main tax to consider when you sell a business or company is capital gains tax. There are various reliefs available, most notably on reinvesting the proceeds.

See
3.21.5

Also
E15 &
VCT
shares
see 4.8 &
4.9

You can claim a form of roll-over relief if you have a gain on the sale of any asset. You must *reinvest* the proceeds in the ordinary voting shares of a 'qualifying company', which is an unquoted company carrying on one or more qualifying trades. Further details are given in Chapter 3.

The reinvestment must be within one year before and three years after your disposal and part or all of your original gain will only be taxed when you sell the new shares. One of the advantages of this relief is that you only need to reinvest the amount of your gain for it to be held over until you dispose of your new shares.

For example, suppose for 1994–5 you have a chargeable gain after indexation relief of £30,000. Within three years after your disposal, you buy ordinary voting shares for £25,000 in a 'qualifying company'. Providing you make the necessary claim, £25,000 of your gain will be held over. In fact, the remaining £5,000 will be covered by your £5,800 annual exemption, if not already used.

11.2.1

3.21.4 *Roll-over relief* in its most widely accepted sense applies where business assets are sold and new ones purchased. Further details are given in Chapter 3. It is important to remember that certain business assets are excluded, such as movable plant and machinery (e.g. forklift trucks).

You should note that this particular relief does not apply to gains made on selling your shares in a company. Instead, it relates to business assets, whether owned by your company or non-incorporated business. The old and new assets must be used in the same business. However, several trades count as one for this purpose.

The relief is very useful where you replace assets used in your business. However, you do not need to replace like with like. For example, you might sell a factory and buy goodwill.

You are allowed to roll-over a gain into a new business asset that is a wasting asset such as a lease (with a predictable life not exceeding 50 years). However, it needs to be replaced with a non-wasting business asset within ten years; otherwise the rolled-over gain becomes chargeable. This rule even applies to a replacement asset which becomes 'wasting' within the ten years, such as a 59-year lease.

The actual relief is in many ways similar to that on reinvestment described above. Thus, the new asset must be acquired within one year before and three years after the disposal of the old asset.

You must claim the relief within six years of the end of the chargeable period in which the disposal of the old asset takes place. The effect is to 'roll-over' all or part of the gain. However, for full relief, the entire proceeds must be reinvested. Otherwise, part of the gain is taxed.

For example, suppose you sell a business asset for £30,000 on which there is a chargeable gain of £10,000. You will need to buy appropriate business assets for at least £30,000 in order to roll-over the whole gain. If the cost is, say, £25,000, the gain will be taxed to the extent of £5,000, unless covered by other relief.

11.2.2

Another capital gains tax relief which is important when you reach middle age is *retirement relief*. This is available at age 55, or younger if you are forced to retire due to ill health. Fuller details are given in Chapter 3.

See 3.21.6

The relief applies both on disposals and gifts of businesses and private 'personal company' shares. Such a company is one in which you hold at least 5% of the voting shares and are a full-time working officer (e.g. director) or employee.

Regarding businesses, the relief applies to gains on chargeable business assets. For companies, a corresponding proportion is relieved, as covered previously. To obtain maximum relief requires at least ten years' ownership. £250,000 of your gain is then tax free and the next £750,000 is relieved at 50%.

11.3   Family Company Takeovers

If your family company is taken over by another company, the gain on your shares can normally be deferred if you accept shares or debentures in exchange. Subject to certain rules, such *paper for paper* exchanges result

See 3.19.2 in your gain being held over until you sell the new shares or debentures. (Any part taken in cash may be taxable.)

An important condition is that the buying company already owns 25% of your company's ordinary shares, or it does so as a result of the takeover.

The Revenue have powers to tax the gain immediately, under anti-avoidance rules. However, you are entitled to apply for Revenue clearance in advance, which you can do on the grounds that the arrangements have been made for *bona fide* commercial reasons, rather than to save tax.

Your professional advisers (probably your accountants) are likely to submit your clearance application. They will need to provide company details, particulars of the deal and copies of various documents, such as company accounts.

If debentures are involved, they will need to be properly drawn up on commercial rather than artificial terms. The duration must also be reasonable and though the Revenue may allow a minimum period of at least six months, a year would be far more comfortable.

Whether or not you should ask for 'paper', or accept it if offered, is an important commercial decision. If the buyers are a large public company, you are to continue working for the group and you wish to have a financial interest, then take some shares. You will be at risk so far as stock market fluctuations are concerned, but you should be able to sell shares when necessary.

With a smaller company buying your own, if you take ordinary shares in exchange, the risk is far greater. Unless the buyer is quoted, you will have difficulty in disposing of your new shares. Thus, only if you are very confident of the new group's prospects should you consider taking its shares.

Often, the most acceptable form of 'paper' is debentures, but you should try to ensure that the terms are satisfactory. Thus, they should give you a fair rate of interest. Also, you should be given the opportunity to redeem over a number of years.

Another vital factor with debentures is that they constitute a safe investment. Thus, for example, they should be secured on other assets or a separate fund established for their repayment.

The main tax savings resulting from taking 'paper' are that you can crystallise your gains when you wish. Furthermore, the same applies to your spouse, assuming that he or she also has had family company shares. (Otherwise, it is worthwhile gifting shares to your spouse prior to the deal.)

Assuming that you (and your spouse) have no other capital gains, you can take enough of the consideration in cash to give chargeable gains equal to your annual exemption (£5,800). However, should you and/or your spouse be entitled to capital gains tax retirement relief, you should take sufficient cash to cover this.

1995–6
£6,000

Then, each subsequent tax year, you can plan to realise enough of your shares or debentures at least to cover the annual exemptions. If you have substantial gains on the deal, you should realise more 'paper' each year, so that you also can use up any balance of your lower and basic rate tax bands.

(This 'paper for paper' relief applies equally to takeovers of one quoted company by another. Thus, you are likely to have encountered it if you are a regular investor in the stock market.)

11.4 Passing on Family Company Shares to your Children

Also see
8.8

If any of your children join you in the family company, you may wish to pass on shares to them. This would particularly apply if they do well. As possibly rather less of a priority, you may also like to give shares to any children who are not working in the company.

The simplest way for you (and your spouse) to transfer shares to your children is by way of gift. Assuming that the shares are in a family trading company which is your 'personal company' (see above), capital gains tax gifts relief is available.

A claim for relief must normally be made by both the giver and the recipient. However, if you transfer the shares to a settlement, only you need elect. Your capital gain, which is based on the market value of the gifted shares, is then held over until they are sold by the recipient. (Similar relief is available where your gift business assets or agricultural property to your children.)

Settlements (see Chapters 6 & 7) can be used for holding shares in your family company. This is of particular value where you are unsure whether your children are sufficiently mature to own them personally. You could normally act as one of the trustees and thus make it unlikely that the trust votes against company policy.

11.4.1

See 6.14 *Accumulation and maintenance settlements* can be used for children who have not yet reached aged 25. Your transfers into such settlements are PETs for inheritance tax purposes. Thus, this tax would only be payable if you die within seven years. You can cover any capital gains tax by a gifts hold-over relief election in the case of shares in a trading company, but not an investment company.

11.4.2

See 7.5 So far as *discretionary settlements* are concerned, inheritance tax is generally payable at half rates. However, if the value of the shares which you settle is low enough, no tax is payable. This is likely to happen where your nil rate band covers the amount transferred; also where business property relief applies.

See 3.21.7 Capital gains tax hold-over relief is available on gifts of any assets to UK discretionary settlements. This includes shares in investment companies as well as trading companies.

11.4.3

See 3.32.5 *Business property relief* greatly eases the inheritance tax burden on transfers of family company shares. As you will note from Chapter 3, subject to the rules, the relief is 50% where your gift is from a holding of 25% or less. Otherwise, 100% relief is obtained.

In calculating your percentage holding, you normally take account of shares held by your spouse. You also include 'related property', such as holdings in settlements in which either of you has an interest in possession and certain charitable trusts. Thus, you need to plan your transfers so as to obtain the maximum benefit.

For example, suppose you have 39% of the shares in your family company and your spouse has 5%. You wish to give 20% to John, who works in the business and 10% to Bill, who does not.

If you first give John his shares, this will attract 100% relief. However, you and your spouse will be left with only 24%. Thus, when you give Bill his shares, only 50% relief is available. However, by giving Bill his shares first, both transfers attract 100% relief.

The relief applies on lifetime transfers that are chargeable and on death. The value of the property concerned is reduced by the appropriate percentage. Bearing in mind that there is no capital gains tax on your assets when you die and your family company shares may well carry 100% relief, the question arises as to why you should gift them during your lifetime.

11.4.4

There are several reasons for *gifting family company shares during your lifetime*, including:

• To encourage those of your children who work in the company, helping them to increase their commitment.

• To guard against the effects of changes in the law in future years – for example, the present business property and gifts reliefs might be reduced or withdrawn.

• By gifting shares you help to spread the company's income among the family, when dividends are paid.

• If the company is sold in the future, the capital gains tax payable in total is likely to be less. This is because more annual exemptions and lower tax bands will be available, unless already used.

● In the event of the company being sold, if you transfer to your family or settle part of the proceeds, this would not normally attract business property relief. Thus, it is more tax effective to gift and settle the shares at an earlier stage.

11.5   Passing other Income Producing Assets to your Children

Since your children are likely to have reached majority by now, you will not be taxed on the income which they earn on assets which you give them. Thus if you are a top rate income tax payer and they are not, any income from assets which you give to them will attract less income tax as a result.

As already mentioned, family company shares are ideal for these purposes. However, where you have no such shares, or do not wish to give them to particular children, quoted shares are suitable. Also, other investments such as gilt-edge securities and corporate bonds are suitable, particularly since they are free of capital gains tax.

As well as likely income tax advantages, there are, of course, inheritance tax benefits from the gifts, since they are potentially exempt (PETs).
See 3.24   However, gift elections cannot be made for capital gains tax purposes.

Thus, it is better to plan your gifts so that your gains remain within your annual exemption. (Note that any loss on shares which you gift to your child can only be used against gains on transfers to that child.) Alternatively, you can gift investments which are not liable to capital gains tax, such as 'gilts' or, indeed, cash.

11.6   Pensions and Life Assurance

See 8.2   As you reach middle age, the importance of *pensions* grows. For one
etc.   thing, you will have fewer years before retirement in which to make contributions. Also, your earnings and tax rates may well be higher so that your tax relief will be more valuable.

Hence there is a strong case for maximising your pension contributions
See 10.8   as covered in Chapter 10 and previously. This may mean making extra

contributions under your company's additional voluntary contribution scheme.

Alternatively, if you use personal pension arrangements, you should pay as much as you can afford each tax year, up to the allowed limits. Do not overlook any available balances of relief from the previous six years. However, if tax rates are about to rise, you might defer some of your unused relief until the increases take effect, so as to save more tax. *See 8.12*

11.6.1

Life assurance is valuable, both as protection and as an investment. If you have a mortgage, you are likely to have some life cover arranged in that connection. Also, if you belong to an occupational pension scheme, you may well be covered for death in service up to four times your final remuneration.

You should keep the position under review. For example, if you change jobs, you may need to take our fresh life cover, to protect your spouse in the event of your death.

The cheapest way to obtain life assurance is through a pension arrangement, since the cost is tax deductible within defined limits. If you use personal pension schemes, part of your premiums can be allocated to life cover. The maximum amount is 5% of your net relevant earnings.

Your life is covered on a 'term' basis. That means that cover ceases once the term expires or you stop paying premiums. (If you require more permanent life cover; this can be provided outside your pension arrangements by means of a whole of life policy.)

However, many personal pension arrangements provide for the value of the fund to be paid to your surviving spouse (or other beneficiaries specified in a trust deed). Once your schemes have been running for some years, this effectively provides a substantial amount of life cover.

11.7 Covering Gifts by Term Assurance

If you make substantial gifts to your children and others, they are normally PETs (potentially exempt transfers). This means that if you die within

See 3.24.1
seven years, the PETs will need to be included in your estate for inheritance tax purposes. The amount to be so included is subject to tapering relief as described in Chapter 3.

Term assurance on your life written in trust is very useful for covering any inheritance tax which may be payable if you die within seven years of making a PET. The donee will normally be liable for the tax and so should receive any policy proceeds.

You should at least cover the full amount of the tax for the first three years and then 80%, 60%, 40% and 20% respectively for the others. This takes account of tapering relief.

For example, suppose you have used up your nil rate band and annual exemption and that the inheritance tax rate stays at 40%. You gift £100,000 to your daughter Jill. In order to cover the potential tax, you should effect term assurance of £40,000 for three years and then £32,000, £24,000, £16,000 and £8,000.

The position regarding gifts within your nil rate band needs watching. The gifts must be cumulated with the rest of your estate for seven years. Thus, although there will be no tax on the gifts themselves, your estate will be deprived of nil rate band equal to the gifts for the seven years.

See 3.24.1
Supposing you gift £150,000 out of your nil rate band, you would need a seven-year policy for £60,000. This is the tax liability of your estate related to the gifted property which will remain for seven years. There will be no tax on the gift itself and so tapering (Chapter 3) has no effect.

11.8   Early Retirement

The following chapter is called 'Retirement' and deals with your retirement and subsequent tax planning. However, you may find yourself retiring during middle age through choice, redundancy, selling your company or illness.

A particular situation with which you may be faced is that your employers offer you early retirement on special terms. Particular points to watch are protection of your pension rights and lump sum compensation payments.

Lump sum payments may be tax free in certain circumstances up to £30,000 as described below. You will need to weigh up the financial inducements against the ease of getting another job and whether you wish to retire.

If you become redundant, there is little choice. However, your employers may be prepared to vary the settlement terms to suit you to some extent. For example, your pension entitlement might be enhanced out of part of what is due to you. Furthermore, up to £30,000 can be paid to you as tax-free compensation, subject to the rules.

Unless otherwise taxed, compensation for loss of office is exempted from tax as to the first £30,000. This includes 'golden handshake' payments on retirement, redundancy and removal from office. Any excess is taxable as earned income. As a rule, payments to you under your service contract will be taxed in any event.

Ex gratia payments on *retirement* or *death* may be taxed under pension scheme rules if relevant. However, Revenue PSO (Pension Schemes Office) approval can be applied for.

Where you have your own business, early retirement might take place because you sell out. In that case, the matters raised earlier in this chapter will be relevant. However, you may agree to remain as an employee or consultant and, provided you have reached 55, you will still be entitled to capital gains tax retirement relief.

See 3.21.6

If your sale is due to ill health, you will be able to obtain capital gains tax retirement relief, even though you have not reached age 55. You will need to show that you are unlikely to become able once again to carry out your previous work. A doctor's certificate is needed and you must claim relief within two years after the end of the tax year in which you make the disposal.

11.9 Settling Abroad

Also see 12.13

One reason for taking early retirement might be that you wish to settle abroad. Alternatively, you may wish to take the opportunity of doing so if you do retire early. Whatever the reasons, the tax effects are most important.

See 2.22 Reference to the table in Chapter 2 will show the effects on your UK tax liability of your settling abroad and thereby ceasing to be domiciled, resident and ordinarily resident here. Broadly, your non-UK income will cease to be taxed in this country and your capital tax position is vastly improved.

Once you are neither resident nor ordinarily resident here, you are not liable for capital gains tax. (An exception is regarding assets which you use here in a trade or profession.) So far as inheritance tax is concerned, the important factor is domicile. If you are no longer domiciled in the *Also see* 3.3 UK, your liability is restricted to assets situated here.

Naturally, you will be subject to the tax regime of your new country, which could be worse than here. Thus, take careful advice on the taxes payable when you choose your new country of residence. However, do not make your choice entirely for tax reasons.

Retiring to a tax haven is particularly important if you are wealthy. You can then reduce your investments in the UK and invest elsewhere, outside the reach of inheritance tax, once you are non-domiciled. You can then make gifts and settlements of non-UK assets and they will not even be *See* 3.23.2 treated as PEPs.

If you want to own some UK assets, you can do so through an offshore company. Provided the company (including its share register) is situated outside the UK, your shares in it are situated overseas. Thus, provided you are non-domiciled, your company is outside the inheritance tax net, even if it owns UK assets.

See 3.3 Regarding capital gains tax, the ideal thing is to take large capital profits only after you cease to be resident and ordinarily resident in the UK. Thus, if you are selling your company, do so after your status has changed. (Even if you are going to live abroad permanently, it is safest to wait until the next tax year.)

See 3.19.2 In some circumstances, it may be possible to take shares or debentures in exchange for shares in your own company, thus holding over the gain.

(Seek Inland Revenue clearance first, giving full details of your plans.) You can then move overseas and sell your new 'paper' when you are neither resident nor ordinarily resident.

It is evident that big tax advantages can be obtained through changing your residence and domicile. The question is how do you do it?

Simply establishing a permanent residence abroad and limiting your UK visits to less than an average of three months each year should normally be sufficient so far as residence is concerned. (You generally need a complete tax year away.) Your residence can be changed fairly easily and ordinary residence follows when it is seen to be permanent. However, you are likely to find that it takes longer to establish a new domicile.

Your domicile is the country which you regard as your natural home and to which you intend to return if you go abroad. Thus you can become non-resident but remain domiciled here. It is a question of creating a series of facts which demonstrate that you now have a new domicile. The following are examples relating to your new country:

  Reside there for a long time
  Purchase a home
  Arrange for your family to be with you
  If you are not married, marry a native of the new country
  Develop business interests there
  Make burial arrangements
  Make a new will under the law of the country
  Exercise political rights
  Although not vital, you could become naturalised
  Have your children educated there
  Resign from UK clubs and associations and join new ones abroad
  Transfer religious affiliations.

11.10 Saving Tax where you are Non-Domiciled even though UK Resident

Ways have just been considered, by means of which you can establish a foreign domicile on settling abroad. In those circumstances, domicile normally follows residence, so that you will first lose your UK residence and then domicile.

The converse position is well worth considering, since non-domicile carries many tax advantages, even where you are UK resident. This position is most likely to arise where you are born overseas and move here. Perhaps the reason is that you have married a native of the UK or you are working in this country for a number of years.

See 2.21.1 In order to retain your non-domiciled status, you need to convince the Inland Revenue that you have strong ties with your original country of domicile. Such ties are as indicated in the previous section. Subject to this, highly favourable treatment is obtained regarding income tax, capital *See 2.22* gains tax and inheritance tax.

11.10.1

So far as *income tax* is concerned, if you are a non-domiciled UK resident, your overseas income will often be dealt with on a remittance basis. This includes much income from investments, employment and businesses abroad. You will only be taxed on the income that you bring in to the UK in the tax year from these sources.

If a source is completely closed one tax year, you can remit the income in the next without any income tax liability. Another way to steer clear of UK income tax on the relevant overseas income is to segregate it from your capital. This might be done by using separate bank accounts for income and capital. The capital account is to be used for remittances.

11.10.2

Capital gains tax is also on a remittance basis, so far as the overseas gains of non-domiciled UK residents are concerned. However, if you are in this position, you will not be able to identify that part of your proceeds which represents the gain.

Planning might include reinvesting your overseas gains and only remitting the proceeds of less successful transactions. In that case, be careful that you use a separate bank account and do not mix the funds you wish to remit with 'capital gain rich' money.

11.10.3

Your *inheritance tax* position as a non-domiciled person will be the same whether or not you are resident here. Liability only extends to those of your assets which are situated in the UK. As discussed above, planning might include building up your overseas assets and using an offshore company to own UK investments.

See 3.23.2

Where you are doubtful as to how long you can justify your non-domiciled status, you should consider how you can best use the advantages. For example, perhaps you should realise gains on profitable overseas investments. Similarly, gifts and settlements of offshore assets are attractive, whilst still outside the inheritance tax net.

11.11   Charitable Gifts

Also see 12.12

Although you might have been making donations to charity for many years, you are likely to have more funds to do this when you reach middle age. Thus a few words about tax reliefs are appropriate relating to gifts to authorised charities.

11.11.1

If you wish to commit yourself for at least four years, you should execute a *deed of covenant* to the charity. You will pay the charity net of 25% tax, which it reclaims. You obtain higher rate tax relief at 15% (40–25) on the gross.

Thus if you covenant to pay the charity £100 gross each year, you will pay £75, net of basic rate tax of £25, which it reclaims. As a higher rate income tax payer, you will have relief at 15% on the gross amount, worth £15.

11.11.2

Gift aid is valuable if you wish to make larger single donations. This applies for gifts of at least £250 net each. (These gifts can also be made by companies.) Your payment is net of basic rate tax, which the charity reclaims. As with covenanted donations, you obtain higher rate relief.

Widespread capital tax reliefs are afforded to gifts to charities. Any such gifts that you make are exempted from capital gains tax. Thus it may be better to gift an asset to a charity rather than sell it yourself at a gain and gift the cash. Of course, you may be able to obtain 'gift aid' if you gift cash, but you must take account of your capital gains tax liability.

Finally, charitable gifts and bequests are free of inheritance tax, both during your lifetime and on death.

Also see
12.14 ## 11.12   Capital Tax Planning

Various aspects of capital tax planning have already been considered in this chapter. Particular subjects covered include capital gains tax reliefs on retirement, reinvestment and passing on family company shares and other assets.

But many other kinds of capital tax planning are likely to be relevant during your middle age. Higher income and greater net worth are often enjoyed during this stage, which create opportunities for tax saving.

11.13   Capital Gains Tax Planning

1995–6
£6,000

See
10.13
So far as capital gains tax is concerned, go for the simple ways of saving tax, so as not to fall foul of anti-avoidance legislation. Certainly employ the special reliefs mentioned earlier and try to use your annual exemption (£5,800) by bed and breakfasting as described in Chapter 10. This technique can also be used to create losses to offset capital gains made in the same tax year.

Thus, if in 1994–5 you sell shares in X plc and thereby realise a capital gain of £10,800, your annual exemption absorbs £5,800, leaving £5,000. You can cover this by selling shares in Y plc at a loss of at least £5,000. If you think that Y plc has good recovery prospects, buy its shares back no earlier than the next day. You will still have the loss to offset against the gain on the X plc shares.

11.13.1

See
3.21.1
Chattels are afforded favourable capital gains tax treatment, as described in Chapter 3. You can dispose of individual items, such as pictures and

furniture, for no more than £6,000 and pay no capital gains tax. If the proceeds are greater, your gain is restricted to five-thirds of the excess.

If you gift chattels to your children and others, the same relief applies, based on the market values of the items concerned. (The gifts would normally be PETs for inheritance tax purposes, unless covered by exemptions.)

Sets generally count as one chattel if disposed of together, but there is often scope for selling individual items within the chattels relief limit. This is a worthwhile exercise, if it can be done without unduly reducing the overall net proceeds.

If you are building up a collection of perhaps antiques or pictures, have regard to chattels relief. Acquire at least some moderately priced items, so that you can sell them within the exemption. In this way, subject to market conditions, you can provide for tax-free funds in future years.

Transferring assets 'pregnant with gain' to your spouse or children before sale is often worthwhile. However, you may have a chargeable gain on transfers to the children. The object is to utilise their annual exemptions and lower rates of tax, unless already used. However, the Revenue have powers to look through artificial schemes and you should avoid these.

11.14   Inheritance Tax Planning

Inheritance tax planning gains in importance as you advance through middle age. Earlier in this chapter, the value of business property relief was illustrated and agricultural property relief is as generous.

This relief is described in Chapter 3. Subject to the rules, the relief is 100% if you have vacant possession or can obtain it within 12 months. Otherwise, the rate is 50% which generally applies for tenanted situations. *See 3.32.5*

The value of regularly using up your annual exemption each year (if you can afford it) is substantial. If your spouse does the same, you are able to pass tangible amounts on to your children. *See 3.26.2*

If your available cash fluctuates from year to year so that funds are not always available, you can still make use of the one-year carry forward facility. This will enable you to make gifts of up to £6,000 every other year.

Do not overlook the exemption each year for gifts up to £250. You can make such gifts to any number of different people, but if you exceed £250 in any case, the gift goes against the £3,000 exemption.

Another important plank in your regular gifts strategy concerns normal expenditure out of income. This is exempt subject to certain rules. You must make regular transfers out of after-tax income, leaving you sufficient income for your normal living standards. An example of how this might be used is where you pay the annual premiums on a life policy written in trust for your children.

See 3.24

To the extent that they exceed the exemptions and reliefs noted above (and others such as on marriage) your transfers are *potentially exempt* (PETs). An important exception is regarding discretionary trusts (below).

However, if you can afford it and you wish to gift larger amounts to your children, the inheritance tax arguments for making PETs are strong. For one thing, the comparatively lenient inheritance tax regime is unlikely to remain for ever.

1995–6
£154,000

Even at present rates, your estate bears 40% once the £150,000 nil rate band has been used. Thus, by gifting, say, £200,000 to your adult children now, £80,000 is saved on the basis that at least this portion of your estate would have attracted 40% tax.

Should you not survive for seven years, the gift will need to be taken into account. However, this contingency can be covered by term assurance, as mentioned earlier in this chapter. Provided you are in good health, the cost is fairly modest.

The above comments about PETs still hold good, even if you leave much of your estate to your spouse. In that case, most or all of the tax is payable on the second death. Regarding any likely eventual inheritance tax liability, you may consider effecting a whole of life policy on a joint life last survivor basis.

11.15   Settlements

If you are uncomfortable about making large outright gifts to your children, consider settling funds instead. If the beneficiaries are under 25 years of age, accumulation and maintenance settlements are an attractive option, as described in Chapter 6.

See 6.14

Discretionary trusts, which are covered in more detail in Chapter 7, are suitable for beneficiaries of all ages. Also, there is far more flexibility. Of course, once you have cleared your nil rate band, inheritance tax is payable at half the full rate. Hence it makes sense for you and your spouse to settle no more than £150,000 plus any unused annual exemption.

See 7.5

1995–6
£154,000

It is a sensible plan to include your widow or widower as a beneficiary in a discretionary settlement in case of need. This avoids the tax disadvantages of including her or him whilst you are still alive.

Finally, by now you may well have grandchildren. If so, you will be able to settle money for them on accumulation and maintenance trusts. Also, any discretionary settlements should be sufficiently widely drawn to include your grandchildren amongst the beneficiaries.

11.16   Changing your Will

Also see
12.15

As you advance through middle age, there will be various occasions when you might need to change your will. For example, you may sell your business, having previously left it to your son. Or perhaps you buy a valuable picture, which you want your daughter to have and thus execute a codicil to your will to this effect.

Or you may become wealthier, perhaps because you have yourself received an inheritance. This will enable you to amend your will, partly to save tax. For instance, you may have left all of your assets to your surviving spouse and now leave £150,000 to your children to make use of the nil rate band.

1995–6
£154,000

11.16.1

This is akin to *generation skipping*, which includes asking your own parents, and others whom you know will leave you money, to leave it to your children instead. Furthermore, if your children are already wealthy, consider leaving money in trust for your grandchildren.

11.16.2

See
12.16
'Generation skipping' can also be effected by *deeds of family arrangement*, which are explained in more detail in Chapter 12. In essence, within two years of the death, the beneficiaries under a will are able to redirect part or all of the estate.

Thus, if you receive, say, £100,000 under your uncle's will, you may have this passed on to your daughter under a deed of variation. The effect is to treat this amount as if it passed to her under the will. No capital gains tax is payable on it, nor inheritance tax on your giving up the bequest.

Also see
12.11
11.17   The Family Home

One of your most valuable assets, if not the major one, is the family home. Furthermore, by this time, you may well have paid off any mortgage and have a substantial source of tax-free money. But remember that the main residence exemption for capital gains tax does not also apply for inheritance tax.

In practical terms, as you get older and the children leave home, you are unlikely to require such a large home. You may thus decide to sell it and buy (or lease) something smaller. The resultant funds will be available for investment or passing on to your family. (This subject is discussed further *See*
12.11 in Chapter 12.)

If you sell a second home, full capital gains tax relief normally only applies if you had elected for it to be your main residence within two years of the second acquisition. However, before making the election, you should make sure that this is in your best interests. It is likely that the gain on your main home will be bigger.

11.18   Investment Aspects

You should avail yourself of the tax-favoured investment opportunities, as outlined in previous chapters. PEPs, TESSAs and certain National

Savings products all have their part to play, as do EIS shares and even single premium insurance bonds. *Also VCTS from 6.4.95*

If your income is high, you may be particularly attracted by the fact that investment in EIS shares will give you 20% tax relief. (This is described in Chapter 9.) However, you must take care that you choose sound investments and that after you have held them for at least the prescribed five years, there is a satisfactory 'exit route'. *See 9.13.6*

Full tax relief at your highest rate is available on investment in Enterprise Zone industrial and commercial buildings. This is because 100% initial allowance applies. However, if you sell within 25 years, a balancing charge may apply. To facilitate smaller investments, Enterprise Zone trusts are available. *See 2.18.7*

11.19   Planning List – Middle Age

• Plan sales and purchases of family company shares to maximise the special capital gains tax reliefs on reinvestment, etc.

• Pass on family company shares and other income-producing assets to your children, availing yourself of the relevant capital taxes reliefs.

• Keep up ample pensions cover and include life assurance.

• Cover gifts by term assurance.

• If you are offered early retirement, carefully assess the tax and other benefits, including compensation payments.

• Settling abroad can attract big tax benefits, particularly if you cease to be UK domiciled and resident.

• If you are non-domiciled although UK resident, maximise the special tax-saving opportunities.

• Make donations so as to save you tax and provide extra for the charity.

- Plan to save both inheritance tax and capital gains tax by fully using the available reliefs.

- Create settlements for your children and grandchildren, including your widow or widower.

- Change your will as necessary and use deeds of family arrangement to save tax by generation skipping, etc.

- Ensure maximum capital gains tax relief on selling family homes and use spare funds for passing on to your family.

- Invest for tax relief but exercise care.

25 110% 100 (1-08) 83 118

26 92   44 86

27 86

28 74   45 33% 146   (5-40)

29 66   46   106   4

30 58   47 30% 168   (6-48)

31 50

32 42   48   120

33 34   49   160   (7-60)

34 60% 118 (2-16) 50 24% 192 (8-68)

35 102   51 22% 216   (9-76)

36 86

37 70   52   236   (10-80)

38 54   53   248   (11-9)

39 43% 120 (3-24) 54 252 (12-96)

40 106

41 82   55 248   (13-104)

42 39% 150 (4-32) 56 236 (14-112)

208   57 206   (15-120)

58

CHAPTER TWELVE

Retirement

12.1

In Shakespeare's words, we have now reached the 'Last scene of all, that ends this strange eventful history...'

But the seventh age is unlikely to be 'second childishness and mere oblivion'. And with both National Health and private medical care available, the description 'sans teeth, sans eyes, sans everything' is going too far.

Perhaps more apt are Lewis Carroll's words spoken by Alice:

> 'You are old, Father William,' the young man said,
> 'And your hair has become very white;
> And yet you incessantly stand on your head –
> Do you think at your age, it is right?'
> 'In my youth' Father William replied to his son,
> 'I feared it might injure the brain;
> But, now I'm perfectly sure I have none,
> Why, I do it again and again.'

Although you will not be sharing with Father William his absence of brain, hopefully you will have a long and active retirement. This chapter deals with related tax planning and subjects covered include:

	Refer to:
Taking your pensions	12.2
Reducing your work load	12.5

12.2 Taking your Pensions

12.2.1

Commutation

Also see
8.2
When you become entitled to your *occupational pension*, you normally have the option of commuting part of this in the form of a tax-free lump sum. The amount is $\frac{3}{80}$ths of your final remuneration for each of your first 40 years of service, or if greater, $2\frac{1}{4}$ times your initial pension before commutation. ('Final remuneration' is capped at £100,000 for these purposes.)

12.2.2

Also see
8.12
Commutation is also available when you commence to draw *personal pensions* and *retirement annuities*. The maximum lump sum is 25% of the fund providing your personal pension. For a retirement annuity the amount is three times the pension subsequently paid; but this is limited to £150,000 for each contract entered into after 16 March 1987.

Thus, substantial tax-free lump sums are normally available under various types of approved pension arrangements. You should opt to receive them, even if you wish to have the largest possible pension.

See
12.10
You can use lump sums to buy annuities, as later described in this chapter. Each periodic payment that you receive will contain a tax-free capital portion. On the other hand, your entire pensions are generally subject to income tax.

Particularly if you retire younger, it is not necessarily advisable to buy an annuity immediately with your lump sum. If you wait a number of years, you will get a better rate. This is because your life expectancy is an important factor in deciding the amount of your annuity. Meanwhile, you could keep the lump sum in a safe investment.

12.2.3

Delaying benefits

Also see 4.7

It does not follow that it is always in your best interests to commence your pension and take your lump sum at the earliest opportunity. If you are able to delay taking these benefits, it may be to your advantage and so you should make inquiries.

Regarding occupational schemes, it is normally necessary to take later retirement and continue making contributions. Whether you wish to do this, or will be allowed to, will depend on the circumstances. (There would normally be greater flexibility with executive pension schemes.)

Personal pension schemes are much more favourable in this respect, as are retirement annuity contracts. You can continue paying premiums until you reach age 75, provided you have net relevant earnings. Even if your earnings are much reduced, you can continue to make contributions, particularly if you have any unused relief from the previous six years.

Even if you cease to pay premiums, you are often allowed to let your policies remain intact for a few years. In this way, the tax-free roll-up continues, although it is wise to ensure that the risk element is not too great. In fact, there may be facilities to switch into safer funds.

Many schemes have arrangements under which you can opt to start parts of your pension at different times. In other words, you may choose for one-fifth of your fund to be so applied in each of five years. In this way, you will be taking a lower pension initially, when you may not need so much. Also, market fluctuations are likely to be averaged out.

The particular rules of any pension schemes to which you belong must be carefully examined. One important point is that it is often sensible to defer taking benefits from a sound scheme. You should consider this, provided you have sufficient income (or spare capital).

12.2.4

State Retirement Pension

1995–6
£3,060.20

When you reach age 60 if you are a woman, or 65 if you are a man, your State Retirement Pension (taxable) will normally commence. The basic amount is £2,995.20 for 1994–5, which will make a modest contribution to your income. However, you can delay taking it for five years and then receive a higher pension.

See App.
16.

If you continue in work, the above still applies regarding your State Pension. Furthermore, from 60 and 65 respectively for women and men, no further National Insurance contributions are generally payable by the employees. However, employer's contributions are still due.

12.5   Reducing Your Work Load

As you reach retirement age, you may relish the prospects of working no longer. On the other hand, you may wish to continue working, but less intensely. As discussed above, this is certainly advantageous for the purposes of maximising your pension cover.

If you have been engaged in a business or profession, you can often continue this on a smaller scale, perhaps from home. This should generate income to supplement your pensions or enable you to delay drawing them. Where you have retired from employment, you may be able to obtain part-time work elsewhere.

See 8.12

Where your earnings are sufficient, it is tax effective to contribute to a personal pension scheme. You obtain relief for your payments and benefit from tax-free roll-up in the fund. Even if you are drawing one pension, you can still contribute to another.

In selecting personal pension schemes, you should satisfy yourself as to such matters as the standing of the company, its investment record and that its charges are moderate. Because the time-span of your new personal pension scheme is likely to be shorter, these factors are particularly important and so, as ever, take good professional advice.

As a director of your family company, it is much easier, in theory, to reduce your work load and carrying on drawing salary. Depending on the exact

212

details of your pension schemes, it should be effective for you to continue your contributions. This is particularly true with money purchase schemes.

12.6 Passing on or Selling your Business or Company

*Also see
11.4*

The advantages of continuing to work, but possibly with a reduced load, are discussed above. The extent to which you can do this is bound up with what happens to the ownership of your company or business.

If you intend keeping your business in the family, it is important that the management continuity is ensured and that the younger members are able to take over the reins. Otherwise, non-family members might be promoted. Either way, it may be appropriate to gift or sell shares as considered in the previous chapter.

Selling shares to your own family is not efficient for inheritance tax purposes. You will not have reduced the value of your estate and you will have cash instead of the shares. Unlike the shares, your cash attracts no inheritance tax relief. Therefore, if you can afford it, gift the shares.

12.6.1

Inheritance tax relief
The inheritance tax aspect is of increasing importance as you grow older. As the law stands at present, you obtain 100% relief on the gift of the whole or part of your business. This applies both to lifetime gifts and to property passing on your death.

*See
3.32.5*

The position regarding unquoted shares is broadly that you need to hold over 25% in order to obtain 100% relief. You include any 'related property' (see Chapter 3), such as shares owned by your wife. For smaller share-holdings the relief rate is 50%. (Further details are given in Chapter 11.)

Regarding agricultural property, the relief is broadly 100% if you have vacant possession or can obtain it within a year. Otherwise, it is 50%.

*See
3.32.6*

Faced with this array of inheritance tax reliefs, you may well ask why you should do anything. Why not keep your business, farm or company until you die? After all, there is no capital gains tax on death.

There are several reasons for action. Firstly, the next generations will be much encouraged by your passing down control to them. Furthermore, if you only qualify for 50% relief, substantial inheritance tax savings will result provided you survive for seven years after the transfers.

Another vital point to consider is that the rules could be changed. Prior to 10 March 1992, the relief rates were only 30% and 50%. Thus they could easily be altered again, especially if there were a change in Government. In other words, the relief percentage applicable at your death could be much lower than now.

12.6.2

Capital gains tax relief

Important capital gains tax reliefs are available when you gift business property, including family trading company shares. As described in *See 11.2* Chapter 11, substantial retirement relief is available, as is hold-over relief on gifts of business assets.

Suppose you gift some family company shares to your son. Retirement relief applies first and then you can both make a hold-over election for the balance. The effect will be to reduce your gain and the base value of the shares for your son by the same amount.

12.6.3

Selling your shares to your company

If you cannot afford to give shares to your family, or perhaps have other reasons for not doing this, a 'buy-back' arrangement might be the answer. (The company must be empowered to buy back its shares by its Articles, which otherwise may need changing.)

Such an arrangement is particularly useful where the company has cash reserves to cover the price. This would work best when your children already hold shares in the company. Then, when you sell back your shares, their percentage holdings increase.

For example, suppose you own 40% of the shares and each of your two sons has 30%. If you sell all of your shares back to the company, each of your sons will then have 50% of the shares in issue. At the same time, you will obtain cash from the company.

Subject to satisfying certain conditions, you will only pay capital gains tax on your share proceeds. Otherwise, you are treated as receiving a distribution on which you pay higher rate tax if applicable to you and the company pays advance corporation tax. The conditions include:

- Yours must not be a quoted company nor a subsidiary of one.

- It must be a trading company or the holding company of a trading group.

- The deal must be to benefit the trade of the company (or 75% subsidiary).

- You must be UK resident and ordinarily resident.

- You need to have owned the shares for at least five years (three in certain cases, such as inheritances).

- If you keep some of your shares, your shareholding must be reduced by at least 25%; and you and your 'associates' must not then hold 30%.

A clearance application can be made to the Inland Revenue and you should do this before going ahead with the 'buy-back'. Full particulars should be provided, including the proposed price, and the Revenue will then confirm whether or not the capital gains tax treatment will apply.

12.6.4

Selling your company
When you reach retirement age, you may well sell your company (or business) outside the family, rather than passing it to your children. Naturally, this is more likely if you do not have children who work in the company.

However, even if you have children who work in the company, they may be happy for it to be sold, provided that they have good service contracts.

Similarly, you might be able to negotiate to remain as a director or receive a consultancy fee for a few years.

See 11.2 The capital gains tax position is most favourable, as described in Chapter 11. To the extent that you receive shares or debentures in exchange for your shares, your gain will be held over. Otherwise, you will normally obtain retirement relief.

See 3.24 If you anticipate getting a good price for your company, consider giving more shares to your children and perhaps grandchildren in advance. This will help to reduce your estate. The gifts will be PETs and be counted for inheritance tax, should you die within seven years.

See 3.32.5 Business property relief will not be available unless the children replace the shares sold with other qualifying assets within three years. However, it should be possible to negotiate values for the gifts which are less than the final sale proceeds.

12.7 Making the most of Age Allowance and Married Couple's Allowance

Also see 2.7–8 The rules for married couple's allowance (MCA) and age allowance offer scope for tax savings for you and your spouse. The reliefs for those under 65 are:

1995–6 £3,525 Personal relief	£3,445 (each)
MCA (goes to husband unless there is an election)	£1,720

1995–6 £14,600 £3,525 If you are 65 and over, you may qualify for the higher allowances as follows. However, they are reduced by £1 for every £2 that your income exceeds £14,200, but not below £3,445 and £1,720 respectively.

			1995–6
Age allowance	65–74	£4,200	£4,630
	75 and over	£4,370	£4,800
MCA	65–74	£2,665	£2,995
	75 and over	£2,705	£3,035

1995–6
£14,600

If your income only moderately exceeds the £14,200 limit, it is worthwhile changing your investments so as to come within the limit. For example, you might go for growth rather than income. Another option could be to transfer investments to your wife or children.

Where your spouse and yourself both have income over £14,200, there is still scope for one of you to obtain the higher allowances. To do this, it is better if the husband reduces his income.

12.8 Example: Planning to receive Age Allowance and Higher MCA

Doris and her husband David are both over 75 and their income and tax are as follows for 1994–5:

	Doris (£)	*David (£)*
Pensions	7,000	8,000
Investment income (gross)	10,000	11,000
	17,000	19,000
Personal relief (restricted)	3,445	3,445
MCA (restricted)		1,720
	13,555	13,835
Income tax: £3,000 at 20%	600.00	600.00
Balance at 25%	2,638.75	2,708.75
	£3,238.75	£3,308.75
Total income tax		£6,547.50

217

If David transfers assets to Doris, so that his income is reduced by £4,800 to £14,200, he will obtain full age allowance and the higher MCA as follows:

	Doris	David
Income	21,800	14,200
Personal/age relief	3,445	4,370
MCA		2,705
	18,355	7,125
Income tax: £3,000 at 20%	600.00	600.00
Balance at 25%	3,838.75	1,031.25
	£4,438.75	£1,631.25
Total income tax	£6,070.00	

Thus, Doris and David have reduced their tax bill by **£477.50**

12.9   Tax efficient investing

Also see 11.18

The investments which carry special tax breaks, as considered in previous chapters, are equally of value now that you have retired. Thus PEPs, TESSAs, National Savings (particularly index linked), EIS shares and Enterprise Zone properties all have their place, the last two if you have a high income.

Also VCTS from 6.4.95

There are several events which are likely to result in your having extra funds to invest. Examples are selling your business and trading down to a smaller house.

Another situation is where you commute part of your pension and wish to buy an annuity, but intend to wait until you are older to get better rates. Depending upon the time scale, PEPs may be suitable for at least part of the lump sum. Another possibility is index linked gilts.

Gilt edge securities are worth considering in general. They have the advantage of being exempt, so far as capital gains tax is concerned. (Corporate bonds have the same exemption.)

Single premium life assurance bonds are also useful investments, in view of the facility for tax-free withdrawals of up to 5% each year. Above that and on termination, if you are a higher rate payer any profit will be charged at 15% (40–25%).

Since you may well need to supplement your income with capital, it is sensible to plan your investments to facilitate appropriate sales as required. If possible, unless you wish to make substantial sales or gifts, aim to keep your capital gains within the £5,800 exemption each year.

1995–6
£6,000

You should remember that a selection of investments is exempt from capital gains tax when you sell. These might usefully be realised, where you have reached the £5,800 exemption limit. They include PEPs, EIS shares held at least five years, Gilts and National Savings bonds.

Finally, you may have some shareholdings which have increased in value and would create high capital gains tax charges if you sold now. Subject to inheritance tax considerations, an answer is to keep the shares until you die, when they will attract no capital gains tax.

12.10   Purchasing Annuities

Another type of tax-efficient investment is the purchased annuity. However, the amount that you can obtain with a fixed capital sum normally increases dramatically with your age. It is thus often advisable to wait until you are older (say over 70) before buying an annuity.

You obtain a steady flow of income and part of this is tax free. This is because it is treated as the repayment of your original capital.

For example, suppose you buy an annuity for £10,000, which produces £100 gross each month. Suppose also that £40 each month is treated as capital. Your monthly cheque will be:

Income element	£60.00*
Less 25% income tax deducted at source	15.00
	45.00
Capital portion (tax-free)	40.00
Monthly cheque	£85.00

* Note that your income element will be liable to higher rate tax if you are in this bracket.

Purchased annuities are the opposite of life assurance policies. Instead of paying regular premiums so that a lump sum is later paid to you or your heirs, you pay a lump sum first, to secure an income, at least for life.

Your annuity can be guaranteed for say five or ten years, even if you die before the period has elapsed. Also, you can arrange for percentage increases to allow for some inflation.

Furthermore, you can arrange an annuity for the joint lives of your spouse and yourself, to continue until the second death. Naturally, guarantees, indexing and joint annuities increase the cost and so the income is less, at least to begin with.

Purchasing annuities plays a vital part in capital tax planning and this is discussed further below. If you buy a basic annuity, the cost is immediately removed from your estate. However, if there is a guaranteed portion remaining when you die, its value must be included.

By providing you with secure income, annuities pave the way for further reductions in your estate by way of lifetime gifts to your family.

However, annuities do reduce the funds available for your heirs. So if you can trust them to look after you and/or your spouse in case of need, there is a case for using your own capital to supplement your income and also make gifts.

12.11 The Family Home

The subject of the family home was touched on in Chapter 11. This is
now considered in more detail. If you and/or your spouse own your home,
various tax-planning arrangements might revolve around it. However,
some ideas are blocked by anti-avoidance rules. *See 11.17*

For example, you cannot normally give your house to your children and
carry on living there. This constitutes a gift with reservation and is not
effective for inheritance tax purposes.

Should your house or flat be too big for you, once your children have left
home, you may wish to sell it and buy something smaller. The capital gain
will be covered by your main residence exemption in normal circumstances and so you are likely to generate some tax-free cash.

Suppose you and your spouse wish to keep the house in the family. One
way is through your respective wills. Make sure that it is owned jointly by
your spouse and yourself as tenants in common. You should then each
leave your share to your children.

When the first of you dies, the other can continue living in the house
and this will not be caught by the reservation of benefit rules. Another
advantage is that at least part of your nil rate bands will be used up by
this arrangement.

Another aspect of planning relating to your home is that some years after
retiring, you may find that you are running short of funds. In this situation,
you might consider a home income plan (HIP), but seek sound advice.

With one form of HIP, you mortgage your property, borrowing no more
than £30,000, and obtain 25% tax relief on the interest. You then buy an
annuity with the loan. This pays the interest and the balance is effectively
your income. When you die, your estate will be responsible for repaying
the mortgage.

Under another type of HIP, you sell all or part of your house for cash. This
is either paid at once or by instalments. You are allowed to live in the
property until you die or move away. You are unlikely to obtain a good
price under this method. However, the house or flat is wholly or partly

removed from your estate for inheritance tax purposes.

12.12   Charitable Gifts

See 11.11 The income tax advantages of making certain types of charitable gifts are outlined in Chapter 11. These will be of value to you during your retirement, particularly if you have a high income. However, it is the capital tax reliefs which are most likely to interest you at this stage in your life.

Gifts to charities are free of capital gains tax and inheritance tax. Thus, any charitable bequests that you make in your will are going to be free of tax. Therefore if your estate would attract a large inheritance tax liability and your family is adequately provided for, the tax burden could be reduced by charitable bequests and lifetime gifts.

Also see 11.9 ## 12.13   Retiring Abroad

The question of settling overseas has been dealt with in the previous chapter, to which reference should be made. However, a few comments are relevant here, since you may well wish to spend your retirement in sunnier climes.

You should obtain details about the tax system of your prospective new country and avoid any that is too confiscatory. The following remarks take no account of any overseas tax.

Provided you take up permanent residence, in due course you will become neither UK resident nor ordinarily resident and eventually non-domiciled.

When you have ceased to be UK resident or ordinarily resident, you can sell UK assets free of capital gains tax. (An exception is where you carry on a trade or profession here through a branch or agency in which the assets are used.)

Once you lose your UK domicile, inheritance tax will only fall on UK situate assets and not overseas ones. (If you wish to retain any UK assets, these can be owned through an offshore company.) You can then gift or bequeath overseas assets to your UK family, free of inheritance tax.

12.14   Capital Tax Planning

Also see
11.12

A number of capital tax planning aspects have been dealt with already in this chapter. These relate to passing on your business or company, investing, annuities, the family home and charitable gifts.

Taking a broad view, as you get older, inheritance tax saving becomes of paramount importance. Capital gains tax can still bite deep, but remember that it does not apply to assets which pass on your death.

1995–6
£154,000

In essence, once your £150,000 nil rate band has been used, every extra pound that you leave when you die attracts inheritance tax of 40 pence. This excludes various reliefs and exemptions, the most important relating to property transferred to your spouse. However, when he or she dies, inheritance tax is payable on that property.

If the 40% charge seems high, remember that when inheritance tax was first introduced in 1986, the top rate was 60%. A future Government may wish to return to this or a higher charge for the top slice of a wealthy estate.

The answer would be for you and your spouse to reduce your estates to such levels that little or no inheritance tax is due. You could do this in several ways. For example, make gifts and settlements, spend capital on living costs and buy annuities.

However, it is not that easy. There are a number of imponderables. How long will you both live? How will your investments fare? Will you need expensive medical care? Also, you need to allow for inflation and special holidays.

Perhaps the best solution is for you to pass down a substantial part of your estate to your family during your lifetime. Hopefully, you have a good pension, since this may well be enough to live on. Otherwise, you will have the income from the balance of your estate, supplemented by capital if necessary. Furthermore, you could buy an annuity.

Should you miscalculate and you or your widow/widower has insufficient funds, your family would normally assist. Of course, they may be unreliable and if you need help some years after the gifts, there might be nothing left. Also, you may wish to remain independent.

At the outset, take careful professional advice. But you as parents will best know your children's characters. If you have doubts, you should retain more of your estate.

In any event, it is wise to continue any medical insurance that you have. (25% tax relief is given on payment, provided you are 60 or more.) This should certainly help to cover most unexpected medical bills and thus reduce the expenses that you bear yourself.

12.14.1

Gifts and settlements
During your retirement you should continue to make gifts out of your annual exemption (£3,000), as should your spouse. You could well gift chattels such as pictures and jewellery. There would be no capital gains tax in view of the £6,000 chattels exemption.

Larger gifts and settlements would normally be treated as PETs. Thus, they would come into the inheritance tax reckoning if you die within seven years. However, this normally should not deter you, unless you are in poor health. Furthermore, the benefit of tapering relief will be available if you survive more than three years.

Another advantage of a lifetime gift is that it is valued at the date of gift rather than death. This would be particularly useful in the case of an appreciating asset. Furthermore, at least some protection is provided where the rules adversely change between the gift and death.

See 6.13 Settlements remain as useful as ever for tax planning during your retirement and the comments in previous chapters hold good. You may wish to create a discretionary settlement to include as beneficiaries your children and perhaps your spouse if he or she survives you.

However, more likely to fit in with the family plans would be one or more trusts in favour of the grandchildren. Provided none are yet 25 years of age, accumulation and maintenance settlements would be suitable. Unlike discretionary trusts, setting one up constitutes a PET (for further detail, *See 6.14* see Chapter 6).

Your spouse and yourself might each create trusts, if you have sufficient spare funds. At the same time, it is normally wise to confine each trust to the children of one set of parents. It will then be an easy matter to make the respective parents the trustees of their children's settlement.

12.15   Varying your will

Also see 11.16

During your retirement, as at other times in your life, it will be desirable for you to alter your will. This may mean complete redrafting, although often an addendum known as a codicil will suffice. At all events, you should consult your solicitor in this connection.

As a rule, your spouse and yourself should arrange that, on the first death, at least the nil rate band passes to others than the survivor. In this way, the benefit (£60,000 tax at present rates) is not lost.

1995–6
£61,600

If there are insufficient other assets, your respective shares in your house can be bequeathed as described earlier in this chapter. Of course, the surviving spouse must be allowed to remain living there.

1995–6
£154,000

Another way of using up the nil rate band is to create a £150,000 discretionary trust by means of your will, should you predecease your spouse. In the trust, your widow or widower is a beneficiary in case of need. These arrangements could be mirrored in your spouse's will.

One reason to change your will is so as to be more exact about which members of the family receive cherished works of art or jewellery. However, if you can gift some of these during your lifetime, tax is likely to be saved as mentioned earlier.

'Generation skipping' should be considered when you are changing your will. (This has been touched on in Chapter 11.) For example, instead of leaving all of your money to your only son, who is now 60 and well off, leave some to each of his two children. They are now 32 and 30, newly married and in need of extra money.

See 11.16.1

A family conference would probably confirm the plan and indeed your son might be the first to suggest it. If he inherited the money, more inheritance tax would be payable on it when he dies. Should the money go to your grandchildren, hopefully they will enjoy it for many years to come.

When your spouse dies, you may be able to retain your existing will without alteration, although changes may be desirable in the new circumstances. However, if you remarry you will need a new will, concerning which the most difficult matter will be reconciling the interests of different members of the family.

12.16   Deeds of Family Arrangement

Your will can be altered within two years after your death by a deed of variation or disclaimer executed by your beneficiaries. Effectively, the will is rewritten and operates for inheritance tax and capital gains tax purposes as from your date of death. Similar rules apply with an intestacy. (Notice to the Inland Revenue is needed within six months of the deed.)

A deed of variation enables the provisions of the will to be widely changed. For example, new beneficiaries can be introduced. On the other hand, a deed of disclaimer involves one beneficiary disclaiming all or part of his interest under the will. The property freed in this way is distributed, in accordance with the will, to the other beneficiaries.

Thus, you may take the view that you can use deeds of variation for some posthumous will adjusting. For example, you are uncertain whether your spouse will have sufficient and so you leave him or her your entire estate.

1995–6
£154,000 However (outside your will) you ask your spouse to consider executing a deed of variation. This would leave the £150,000 nil rate band to the children, depending on funds being available.

Unfortunately, this plan has various drawbacks. Firstly, the law may have changed before the deed is executed. Then, the arrangement puts pressure on the surviving spouse and the children may be reluctant to mention the matter.

If you have sufficient funds, a better plan might be to bequeath £150,000 to the children and ask them to redirect money to your spouse in case of need. This could be done by deed of variation, loan or gift.

Deeds of variation can be used in many different ways. For example:

- You inherit money from an elderly uncle and wish it to go to your children.

- You wish to incorporate an accumulation and maintenance trust for your grandchildren into the will of your late spouse.

- A high inheritance tax bill results from your spouse leaving too much to your children and you wish that part goes back to you. (You intend to use it for lifetime gifts.)

- Your spouse leaves you all her estate and you wish that £150,000 goes to your children.

12.17 Example: Deed of Variation

Jack dies and leaves £500,000. Of this, £200,000 is to go to Jill, his widow, and £100,000 to each of his three sons, Tom, Dick and Harry. Inheritance tax is payable as follows:

Value of Jack's estate		£500,000
Less bequest to Jill (free of inheritance tax)		£200,000
		£300,000
	£150,000 at NIL %	
Inheritance tax payable	£150,000 at 40%	£60,000

The family's solicitor advises them to effect a deed of variation. None of the sons need all of their legacies and so they effect a deed reducing their shares to £50,000 each. Thus, Jill now has £350,000 and the revised inheritance tax is:

Value of Jack's estate		£500,000
Less bequest to Jill (free of inheritance tax)		£350,000
		150,000
Inheritance tax payable	£150,000 at NIL %	NIL

Thus, the deed of variation removes the original £60,000 inheritance tax liability altogether. Furthermore, Jill is now able to gift the extra £50,000 to each son out of her annual exemptions and otherwise as PETs. This would achieve the original objectives of Jack's will, with maximum tax savings, if Jill survives for seven years.

So the seven ages of tax planning even extend beyond your death. Under present law, your heirs can make valuable tax savings with deeds of family arrangement.

12.18 Planning List – Retirement

• Examine whether you can delay taking any of your pensions and generally commute part, keeping this for possible later annuity purchase.

• Plan to phase yourself out of your business or company whilst still making pension contributions.

• Sell or gift your business in the most tax-efficient way.

• Make the most of your married couple's allowance and age allowance by such means as asset transfers.

• Fully use the openings for tax-efficient investing.

• Purchase annuities if appropriate to provide a partly tax-free income stream and reduce your estate for inheritance tax purposes.

• Consider the different tax-planning options concerning your family home.

• Make charitable gifts in the most tax-efficient way and to reduce your estate.

• Investigate the tax system of any country to which you wish to retire and structure your affairs to save UK tax.

• Plan your affairs so as to reduce capital gains tax and inheritance tax.

- Revise your will as necessary, so as to minimise inheritance tax.

- Execute deeds of variation and disclaimers within two years of a death, so as to improve the inheritance tax position.

One Word More on the Seven Ages of Tax Planning

That concludes our journey through the 'seven ages'. On the way you are likely to have been able to identify many tax-saving ideas appropriate to your circumstances. But ensure that your tax-planning strategy is as flexible as possible. It is impossible to predict exactly what will happen in the future.

As Benjamin Franklin said, '... in this world nothing is certain but death and taxes'. This book can offer help concerning only the inevitability of the latter but not the former. Its aim has been simple: to help you cut your tax bill.

APPENDIX

Rates and Reliefs at a Glance

NOTE: This Appendix mainly provides information regarding 1994–5. For details concerning 1995–6, reference should be made to Chapter 4, which deals with the November 1994 Budget.

Income Tax

1995–6
see 4.2.1 **1. Income tax rates for 1994–5**

Slice of income	Rate	Total income (after allowances)	Total tax
3,000 (£0–3,000)	20%	3,000	600
20,700 (£3,000–23,700)	25%	23,700	5,775
Remainder	40%		

2. Personal reliefs for 1994–5

1995–6
see 4.2.3

Type	Circumstances	Relief
Personal allowance	Single	£3,445*
Life assurance relief	Policy effected before 14 March 1984 on your own or wife's life – deduction from premium	$12\frac{1}{2}$% of premiums
**Additional personal allowance for children		£1,720*
Blind person's allowance		£1,200
Age allowance	Age 65–74 – Single	£4,200*
	Age 75 or over – Single	£4,370*
	Reduced by £1 for every £2 of excess income over £14,200 down to personal reliefs level	
**Married couple's allowance	Age under 65	£1,720*
	Age 65–74	£2,665*
	Age 75 and over	£2,705*
**Widow's bereavement allowance		£1,720*

*These allowances will be increased for future years in line with the retail price index (unless the Treasury otherwise orders, as it did this year).
**These allowances are restricted to 20% for 1994–5 and 15% for 1995–6.

3. UK securities on which interest may be paid gross to non-residents

Subject to a claim being made to the Inland Revenue, interest on the following is free of UK tax where the securities are owned by individuals not ordinarily resident in the UK:

$2\frac{1}{2}$%	Treasury Loan, 2024	8%	Treasury Loan, 2003
$3\frac{1}{2}$%	War Stock 1952 or after	8%	Treasury Loan, 2013
$4\frac{1}{8}$%	Treasury Loan, 2030	$8\frac{1}{2}$%	Treasury Loan, 2007
$4\frac{3}{8}$%	Treasury Loan, 2004	$8\frac{3}{4}$%	Treasury Loan, 1997
$4\frac{5}{8}$%	Treasury Loan, 1998	$8\frac{3}{4}$%	Treasury Loan, 2017
$5\frac{1}{2}$%	Treasury Stock, 2008–12	9%	Conversion Stock, 2000
6%	Treasury Loan, 1999	9%	Treasury Loan, 2008
$6\frac{3}{4}$%	Treasury Loan, 1995–8	9%	Convertible Loan, 2011
$6\frac{3}{4}$%	Treasury Loan, 2004	9%	Treasury Loan, 2012
7%	Treasury Loan, 2001	$9\frac{1}{2}$%	Treasury Loan, 1999
7%	Treasury Conv., 1997	$12\frac{3}{4}$%	Treasury Loan, 1995
$7\frac{1}{4}$%	Treasury Loan, 1998	$13\frac{1}{4}$%	Treasury Loan, 1997
$7\frac{3}{4}$%	Treasury Loan, 2006	$13\frac{1}{4}$%	Exchequer Loan, 1996
$7\frac{3}{4}$%	Treasury Loan, 2012–15	$15\frac{1}{4}$%	Treasury Loan, 1996
8%	Treasury Loan, 2002–06	$15\frac{1}{2}$%	Treasury Loan, 1998

4. Pensions – Contribution limits

Age at start of year of assessment	Personal pensions	Retirement annuities
	% of net relevant earnings	
Under 36	17.5	17.5
36–45	20	17.5
46–50	25	17.5
51–55	30	20
56–60	35	22.5
61 and over	40	27.5

5. Tax remission limits from 17 February 1993

Where you submit complete tax returns but receive no assessments due to Inland Revenue error, it is their practice to remit part of the tax as follows:

Gross income limits	Fraction of arrears collected
£15,500	None
18,000	$\frac{1}{4}$
22,000	$\frac{1}{2}$
26,000	$\frac{3}{4}$
40,000	$\frac{9}{10}$
above 40,000	All

6. Penalties

The following are examples of some of the maximum penalties:

Offence	Penalties
Failure to submit personal tax returns (1).	£300 plus £60 per day after a court declaration.
Failure to submit return continuing beyond tax year following that in which issued (1).	Additional penalty of up to the amount of tax on income and gain, for year. However, if there is no assessable income or gains, the maximum *total* penalty is £100.
Incorrect returns (2).	100% of tax lost.
Assisting in the preparation of incorrect returns or accounts (2).	£3,000
Supplying incorrect information to the Revenue (2).	£3,000

Offence	*Penalties*
Failure to give notice of liability to tax.	From 6 April 1989 the penalty is the amount of tax if notice is more than one year overdue.
Failure to make (when required) a return of information for the Revenue (2).	£300 plus £60 for each additional day in default.
Late submission of employers year-end PAYE returns.	Initial penalty of up to £1,200 per 50 employees and £100 per 50 employees per month for further delays up to one year; beyond which up to 100% of tax underpaid or paid late.
Fraudulent or negligent certificate of non-liability to tax re building society or bank deposit (3).	Up to £3,000.
False statement made by sub-contractor to obtain exemption from tax deduction.	£5,000.

Note: Starting dates:
      (1) 6 April 1989

(2) 27 July 1989
(3) 25 July 1991.

7. Capital Gains Tax

1995–6
see 4.11

Rate (individuals)	20%/25%/40%
Annual exemption (individuals etc)	£5,800
(available separately for husband and wife)	
Annual exemption — disability trusts	£5,800
other trusts	£2,900

8. Retail prices index (adjusted)

	1982	1983	1984	1985	1986	1987	1988	1989	1990	1991	1992	1993	1994
January		82.6	86.8	91.2	96.2	100.0*	103.3	111.0	119.5	130.2	135.6	137.9	141.3
February		83.0	87.2	91.9	96.6	100.4	103.7	111.8	120.2	130.9	136.3	138.8	142.1
March	79.4	83.1	87.5	92.8	96.7	100.6	104.1	112.3	121.4	131.4	136.7	139.3	142.5
April	81.0	84.3	88.6	94.8	97.7	101.8	105.8	114.3	125.1	133.1	138.8	140.6	144.2
May	81.6	84.6	89.0	95.2	97.8	101.9	106.2	115.0	126.2	133.5	139.3	141.1	144.7
June	81.9	84.8	89.2	95.4	97.8	101.9	106.6	115.4	126.7	134.1	139.3	141.0	144.7
July	81.9	85.3	89.1	95.2	97.5	101.8	106.7	115.5	126.8	133.8	138.8	140.7	144.0
August	81.9	85.7	89.9	95.5	97.8	102.1	107.9	115.8	128.1	134.1	138.9	141.3	144.7
September	81.9	86.1	90.1	95.4	98.3	102.4	108.4	116.6	129.3	134.6	139.4	141.9	145.0
October	82.3	86.4	90.7	95.6	98.5	102.9	109.5	117.5	130.3	135.1	139.9	141.8	145.2
November	82.7	86.7	91.0	95.9	99.3	103.4	110.0	118.5	130.0	135.6	139.7	141.6	145.3
December	82.5	86.9	90.9	96.0	99.6	103.3	110.3	118.8	129.9	135.7	139.2	141.9	146.0

Note At January 1987 the index base was changed to 100.0 and the above table shows figures before that date adjusted to the same base.

9. Companies

Full corporation tax rate	33%
Small companies rate	25%
limit for full relief for single company	£300,000
limit for marginal relief for single company	£1,500,000
Marginal rate	35%
Advance corporation tax (ACT) rate	$\frac{1}{4}$th

10.   Inheritance Tax

Annual exemption £3,000

*1995–6
see 4.13* **11. Inheritance tax rate after 9 March 1992**

Slice of cumulative chargeable transfers	Cumulative total	% on slice	Cumulative total tax
The first			
£150,000	£150,000	Nil	£Nil
The remainder		40	

Note this table applies from 10 March 1992 to 5 April 1995

12. Tapering relief

Where an individual dies within seven years of making a potentially exempt transfer (PET) a proportion of the full tax is payable as follows:

Death in years	%
1–3	100
4	80
5	60
6	40
7	20

13.   Stamp Duty

Exemptions from stamp duty

Transfers of Government Stocks ('Gilts')

Transfers of units in certain authorised unit trusts invested in UK government securites, etc

Tranfers of short term loans (no more than five years)

Transfers of certain fixed rate non-convertible loan stocks

Transfers of bearer loan capital

Transfers of certain non-sterling loans raised by foreign governments or companies

Conveyances, transfers or leases to approved charities (FA 1982 S129)*

Conveyances, transfers or leases to the National Heritage Memorial Fund*

Transactions effected by the actual operation of law

Documents regarding transfers of ships (or interests in them)

Transfers brought about by will (testaments and testamentary instruments)

Articles of apprenticeship and of clerkship

Customs bonds, etc

Certain legal aid documents

Contracts of employment

Certain National Savings documents

Deeds of Covenant and bonds

Policies of insurance and related documents (excluding life assurance up to 31 December 1989)

One life assurance policy which is substituted for another according to the rules (FA 1982 S130)

Transfers (and issue) of certain EC Loan Stocks

Transfers of Treasury guaranteed stock

Property put into unit trusts (0.25% prior to 16 March 1988) (FA 1988 S140)

Agreement pursuant to Highway Acts

Appointment, procuration, revocation

Letter or power of attorney

Deeds not liable to other duties no longer liable to 50p duty

In Scotland, resignation, writ, etc

Warrants to purchase Government stock, etc (FA 1987 S50)

Transfers to a Minister of the Crown or the Treasury Solicitor (FA 1987 S55)

* Not treated as duly stamped unless they have a stamp denoting not chargeable to duty

14. *Ad valorem* stamp duties

	Rate
Capital duty (1% before 16 March 1988)	Nil
Conveyance or transfer on sale other than share transfers*	1%
Share transfers (generally including unit trusts) from 27 October 1986	$\frac{1}{2}$%
Certain non-exempt loan transfers after 31 July 1986	$\frac{1}{2}$%
Exchanges or partitions of freehold land	1%
Inland bearer instruments (3% before 27 October 1986)**	$1\frac{1}{2}$%
Overseas bearer instruments**	$1\frac{1}{2}$%
Conversion of UK shares into depositary receipts	$1\frac{1}{2}$%
Lease premiums	1%

Leases: *Ad valorem* duty on rents

Term	Annual rent	Duty for every £50 or part thereof
Not exceeding 7 years	Not exceeding £500	Nil
or indefinite	exceeding £500	50p
7–35 years	—	£1
35–100 years	—	£6
over 100 years	—	£12

(Where the rent does not exceed £500 a sliding scale applies.)

	Amount assured:	
Life assurance policies – up to 31 December 1989	Up to £50	Nil
	£50–£1,000	5p per £100 or part
	Over £1,000	50p per £1,000 or part
After 31 December 1989		Nil
Superannuation annuity contract or grant	—	5p per £10 annuity or part
After 31 December 1989		Nil

* Includes land, etc. For most categories including houses, no duty is payable if the value is certified at no more than £60,000.
** Bearer loan capital exempt.

15. Value Added Tax

1995–6
see 4.14

Standard VAT rate	17.5%
Rate on domestic fuel and power to 31 March 1995	8%
Registration threshold after 30 November 1994	
(annual turnover)	£45,000

16. Social Security

National Insurance Contributions

1995–6
see 4.15

	Tax year			
	1994–5		*1993–4*	
	Employee	*Employer*	*Employee*	*Employer*
'Class 1' – employees aged 16 & over:				
Lower earnings limit (LEL) pw	£57.00		£56.00	
Upper earnings limit (UEL) pw	£430.00		£420.00	
(a) earnings less than LEL:	Nil	Nil	Nil	Nil
(b) earnings LEL or more and contracted out: up to LEL on balance up to UEL				
(c) earnings at least LEL and contracted in: on earnings up to UEL	See Table below			
'Class 2'—self-employed pw	£5.65*		£5.55*	
'Class 3'—voluntary pw	£5.55		£5.45	
'Class 4'—self-employed earnings related	7.3% on annual earnings between £6,490 & £22,360		6.3% on annual earnings between £6.340 & £21.840	
*Lower earnings limit	£3,200		£3,140	

Class 1 National Insurance contributions

1993–4 Employee	Not contracted-out	Contracted-out	1994–5 Employee	Not contracted-out	Contracted-out
Weekly earnings			Weekly earnings		
below £56	Nil	Nil	below £57	Nil	Nil
Earnings above £56			Earnings above £57		
0–£55.99	2%	2%	0–£56.99	2%	2%
£56–£420	9%	7.2%	£57–430	10%	8.2%
£420 or more	No further liability		£430 or more	No further liability	

1993–4 Employer Weekly earnings	Not contracted-out %	Contracted-out % First £56	Excess over £56
Under £56.00	Nil	Nil	Nil
£56.00– 94.99	4.6	4.6	1.6
95.00–139.99	6.6	6.6	3.6
140.00–194.99	8.6	8.6	5.6
195.00–420.00	10.4	10.4	7.4
over £420.00	10.4	10.4	{ 7.4 on £364 10.4 on excess

1994–5 Employer Weekly earnings	Not contracted-out %	Contracted-out % First £57	Excess over £57
Under £57.00	Nil	Nil	Nil
£57.00–99.99	3.6	3.6	0.6
100.00–144.99	5.6	5.6	2.6
145.00–199.99	7.6	7.6	4.6
200.00–430.00	10.2	10.2	7.2
*over £430.00	10.2	10.2	{ 7.2 on £373 10.2 on excess

Glossary

The following is an explanatory list of some of the more usual terms you may encounter both within this book and elsewhere.

Ad valorum duties	Duties, such as stamp duty, that are charged as a percentage of the subject matter.	*See Appendix 14*
Advance corporation tax	Tax paid by companies on their distributions, such as dividends, and set against their full (mainstream) corporation tax.	*See 2.25*
Back duty	Tax under-assessed for past years, usually because of evasion.	*For penalties see App. 6.*
Basic rate	Income tax at 25%.	
Business Expansion Scheme (BES)	Government scheme for giving Tax relief for investment in the shares of smaller companies up to 31 December 1993.	*See 2.6 (by Basic Rate)*
Chargeable gain	A gain accruing to a taxpayer computed in accordance with the capital gains tax legislation.	*See 3.2 et seq*
Chargeable transfer (for inheritance tax)	The decrease in your net assets brought about by an asset transfer less certain exemptions.	*See 3.23.1*

See 9.13.6	Claw-back	The loss of previously received relief, such as where you sell EIS shares within five years.
	Close company	A company which is closely controlled by normally no more than five shareholders and their associates.
	Close investment holding company (CIC)	A close company which is not a trading company, nor a member of a trading group, nor a property investment company.
	Current use value	The value of land and buildings on the basis that it can only be used in accordance with existing planning consents.
See 2.18.2	Current year basis	The assessment basis to apply uniformly for income tax from 1997–8 at the latest.
See 2.21.1	Domicile	The country which you consider to be your natural home.
	Earned income	Income from a person's mental or physical labour and some pensions.
See 9.13.6	Enterprise investment scheme (EIS)	Government scheme which took over from the BES on 1 January 1994 and gives 20% tax relief on investment in the shares of certain smaller companies.
	Ex gratia payment	One made without any liability.
	General Commissioners	Lay people appointed to hear tax appeals.
See 2.6	Higher rate tax	Income tax at rates higher than basic rate, currently 40%.
See 3.13	Indexation allowance	Capital gains tax relief to compensate for inflation.

242

Interest in possession	The entitlement to receive the income of a settlement.
Lower rate tax	Income tax at the lowest rate, at present 20%. *See 2.6*
Mainstream corporation tax	The total corporation tax of a company, based on its adjusted accounts profit. *See 2.24*
Married couple's allowance (MCA)	Income tax relief of £1,720 (or more for certain older people) given where married couples are living together. *See 2.7–8*
Ordinary residence	The country where you reside in the ordinary course of your life. *See 2.21.3*
Partnership	The relationship existing between persons in business together with the object of making profits. *See 2.20*
Personal allowance	The main deduction from your total income being £3,445 and sometimes higher for those over 65 (age allowance). *See 2.7–8*
Personal equity plan (PEP)	Share purchase scheme saving income tax and capital gains tax on purchases of up to £9,000 each fiscal year. *See 9.13.4*
Potentially exempt transfer (PET)	A gift between individuals or to certain trusts which are clear of inheritance tax unless the donor dies within seven years. *See 2.24*
Profit related pay (PRP)	Incentive pay to employees attracting only limited income tax up to certain limits. *See 8.4.3*
Residence	The country where you are treated as living for tax purposes. *See 2.21.2*
Self-assessment	The system which will operate from 1996–7 under which you will play *See 2.5*

		a larger part in computing your tax liability.
	Special Commissioners	Professionally qualified civil servants appointed to hear tax appeals.
See 1.2	Tax avoidance	Legally arranging your affairs to reduce your tax liability.
See 1.2	Tax evasion	Saving tax illegally.
	Tax credit	Overseas or UK tax often deducted at source, which you can set off in arriving at your final liability.
See 9.13.5	Tax exempt special savings account (TESSA)	Building society or bank savings account with tax-free interest.
See 6.13	Trust (or settlement)	Where assets are held by one or more trustees for the benefit of others
	Unearned income	Income from investments rather than earned income (see above).
See 2.5	Year of assessment	Fiscal year (ending 5 April) for which tax is payable.

Index

Note: the references in the index refer to section numbers; there is no reference to page numbers. App = Appendix.

Index